Irish Hands

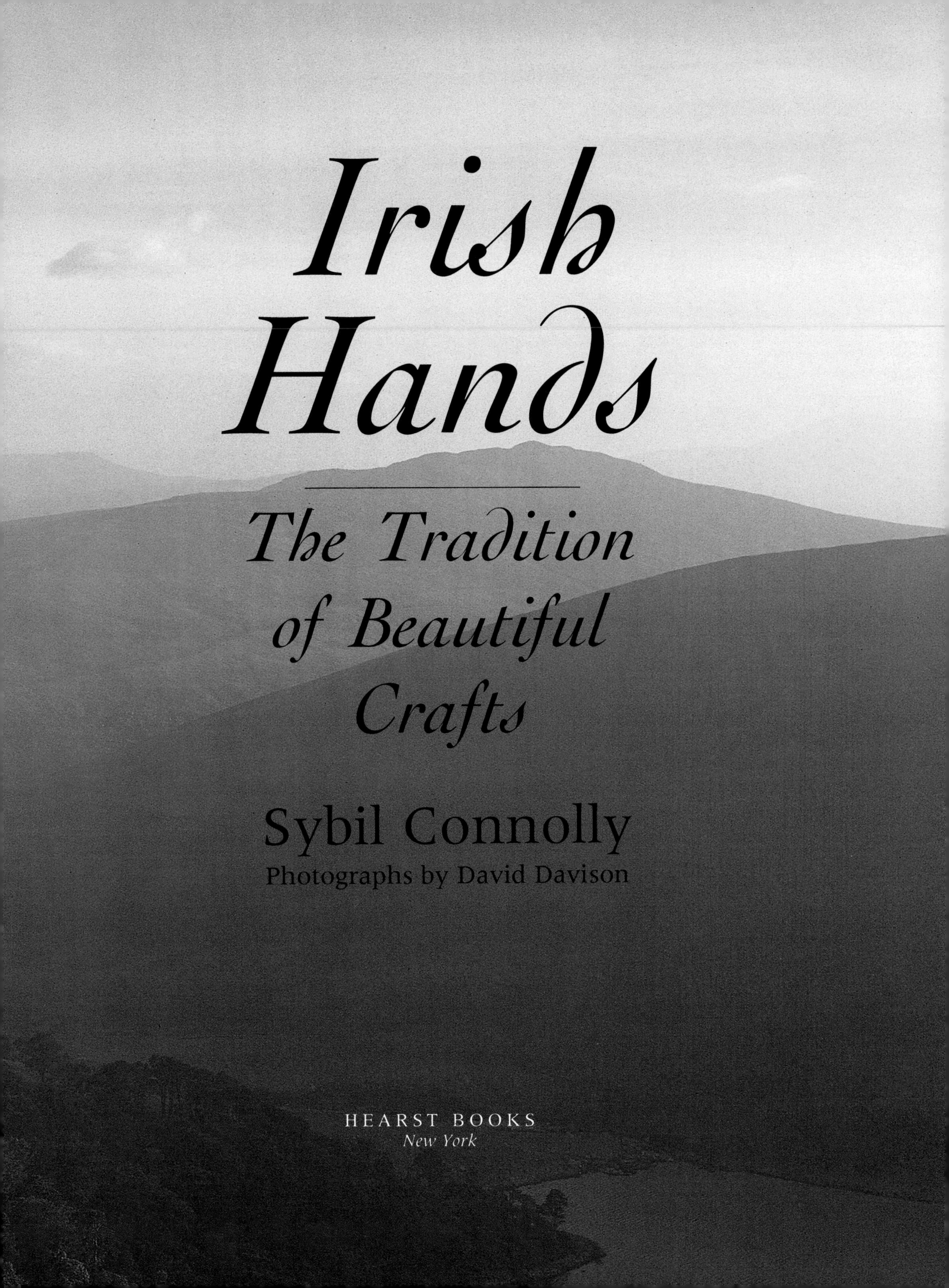

Irish Hands

The Tradition of Beautiful Crafts

Sybil Connolly

Photographs by David Davison

HEARST BOOKS
New York

Library of Congress Cataloging-in-Publication Data

Connolly, Sybil.
    Irish hands : the tradition of beautiful crafts / Sybil
Connolly : photographs by David Davison. — 1st ed.
        p.   cm.
    Includes index.
    ISBN 0-688-11011-8
    1. Handicraft—Ireland.   2. Handicraft—Northern Ireland.
3. Artisans—Ireland.   4. Artisans—Northern Ireland.
I. Davison. David,   II. Title.
TT59.C66   1994
745'.09415—dc20   94-6970
                                                 CIP

Printed in the United States of America

First Edition

1 2 3 4 5 6 7 8 9 10

BOOK DESIGN BY RICHARD ORIOLO
MAP BY JEFFREY L. WARD

Dedication: A Tribute to Muriel Gahan

I am honored that Dr. Muriel Gahan has allowed me to dedicate this book to her.

It is safe to say that no one has done more to promote and nurture traditional Irish handcrafts than Muriel Gahan; in conversation with craftspeople all over Ireland, it is obvious that she is loved and respected. It would be difficult to pinpoint a particular contribution she has made to further the cause of Irish handcrafts; during her long life (she was born in 1897, in the reign of Queen Victoria), there have been many milestones, certainly the opening of the Country Shop in the basement of a Georgian house on St. Stephen's Green, Dublin, in 1930, was one of them.

In the early part of the twentieth century as the Irish economy gradually began to improve, some crafts went into temporary decline—they had become symbols of poverty identified with difficult times. The opening of the Country Shop changed all of that. It was the first showcase for traditional Irish handcrafts and as such was an immediate success.

Homespun and handwoven tweeds in a glorious array of weaves and colors, knitwear, pottery, handwoven floor rugs, wickerwork, baskets woven from willow or rushes gathered from Irish lakes and rivers were all on permanent display, and created a resurgence of interest in the work of the craftsman/woman.

Today, more than half a century later, what could be described as the successor to the Country Shop, the annual Craft Fair, renamed Showcase Dublin, held every January since 1977 in the premises of the Royal Dublin Society, attracts buyers from around the world. The sales from the most recent fair amounted to approximately £14 million, half of which were export orders.

Another important milestone in the preservation of Irish crafts initiated by Muriel Gahan and a group of women (most of them her friends and co-workers) was the formation of an organization to manage the Country Shop and to carry out a country-wide production program in remote parts of Ireland, in order to recognize and help the isolated spinners and weavers. The Irish Countrywomen's Association, as it was called, has continued to play a prominent part in the preservation of traditional crafts, and through its subsidiary, The Co-operative Society of Country Markets, has opened up new markets for a wide range of country products.

It had been a long-cherished dream of Muriel's that one day there would be a permanent residential countrywomen's college, where the encouragement and development of traditional Irish crafts, together with Irish music, art, and literature, would always have a place. Perhaps Muriel Gahan's greatest contribution was her ability to influence Dr. Emory Morris, president of the W. K. Kellogg Foundation, to fund a Country Women's College. The dream became a reality—the Irish Countrywomen's Association got their college— An Grianan, a fine nineteenth-century house surrounded by many acres of its own land, a gift from the W. K. Kellogg Foundation.

This wonderful gift was to be the first experience of the Kellogg Foundation's boundless goodwill and generosity toward furthering the cause of Irish handcrafts, a generosity which has continued from that time onward.

The Royal Dublin Society

I have been always aware that the Royal Dublin Society is a remarkable organization, but it wasn't until I began to research this craft book that I came to realize the full extent of its munificence.

Beginning in 1731, the year the society was founded, it has, without cessation, given financial and other support to the development of Irish crafts. In 1968 the society initiated a national craft competition, an exhibition which is held every year at the August Horse Show. The entrants now number close to one thousand.

When the Craft Council was founded in 1971, the Royal Dublin Society was a founder member; they provided headquarters for the council, and, until the latter received a government grant in 1976, they paid for all secretarial and other expenses.

Contents

Dedication: A Tribute to Muriel Gahan   v

Introduction   viii

In and On the Irish House

Textiles

Precious Metals

The Irish Table

Leatherwork

Introduction

When it was suggested that I write a book featuring some of Ireland's handcrafts, the idea was immediately appealing. For much of my adult life I have had the pleasure of working with many of Ireland's craftspeople, who through their work keep alive the centuries-old tradition of Irish crafts.

My first task (not an easy one) was to decide, within the restrictions imposed by time and space, which of the many crafts practiced in Ireland today would be featured in this book. After some soul-searching, I came to the decision to write about the crafts that I was most familiar with. Even so, of those recorded here there are many more exponents, almost all of whom produce work of interest and quality.

My second task was to research the origins of the chosen crafts; in doing so it soon became obvious that the history of Irish crafts is a microcosm of the history of Ireland. Research also helped to clarify one of the distinctions between art and craft: Whereas the business of art is to provoke, even incite, crafts have no such responsibility, having come into existence mainly for utilitarian purposes.

Ireland is best known for its literary and musical traditions. The physical isolation of Ireland from Europe and the spareness and frugality of rural Irish life during the nineteenth and early twentieth centuries played a large part in creating and preserving those traditions. Deprived of material benefits, when the day's work was done, people would gather around the peat fire and make their own entertainment. They coped with their poverty by escaping into their dreams and imaginations, from which came a language rich with the mythologies of fantasy and hope. The double edge of sorrow and joy is very Irish; it runs through all of our songs and poetry, and in beautiful, remote places like Connemara and areas of Donegal, it even seems reflected in the landscape. Isolation also played an important role in preserving Ireland's crafts. As the men indulged in storytelling, the women of the house sat in the flickering light of the peat fire, spinning, knitting, or making lace, pausing when necessary to instruct their daughters.

In the wake of the destitution incurred by the Great Famine of 1849, political and religious differences were set aside as the people of all denominations worked together to alleviate the burden of those whom the famine had made most vulnerable. Like a phoenix rising from the ashes, lace schools, such as the ones started by the nuns at the St. Louis Convent in Carrickmacross, were founded all over Ireland to teach lacemaking and provide work for the wives and daughters of the beleaguered farmers. Carrickmacross lace, appliquéd with stitches so fine that they are impossible to see without the aid of a magnifying glass, is still made as it was more than a century ago. The only concession to the twentieth century is the range of colors now available. Traditionally, the lace was always black, white, or cream, but during the early sixties, the nuns gave their blessing to my suggestion of making the lace in an array of colors. Lavender blue, blush pink, lime green, and coral were just a few of the colors that inspired a collection of cocktail and evening dresses, each one looking good enough to eat.

For me, it was inevitable that working on this book would evoke a thousand memories of the time when Ireland was making inroads into the world of high fashion. Irish lace and linen already had an appreciative audience, and Irish tweed was best known for its durability and earthy colors, but in order to be suitable for haute couture, Irish tweeds would have to be considerably lighter in weight and color. I worked with Magee and Company of Donegal and their weavers to create a collection of pastel-colored lightweight fabrics that subsequently enjoyed a considerable success and were named Whitewashed Tweeds by Carmel Snow, the legendary fashion editor of *Harper's Bazaar*.

It is difficult to imagine now, but just thirty-five or forty years ago, weaving Irish tweed was literally a cottage industry. We traveled from weaver to weaver explaining to and showing them what we wanted and needed for our most discriminating customers. The looms were set up in roughly built, stone-walled structures leaning against the side of the cottage where the weaver and his family lived. The cottages lay in the sweeping brow of the hills on plots of land coaxed from the reluctant bog and kept from its sodden clutches by constant labor. The weaver inevitably kept a cow to provide the family's milk supply and a small area for growing potatoes and other vegetables. Their frugal existence in no way curtailed the hospitality shown to us as we

made our stops throughout Donegal. At the end of every working session, strong black tea accompanied by freshly baked wholemeal bread spread thickly with golden-yellow homemade butter was lavished upon us and usually partaken of sitting around the hearth fire. Sometimes a cast-iron pot shaped like a witch's caldron hung over the fire. In it giant potatoes heaved like a school of whales. Eaten with freshly churned butter, nothing since has tasted so good.

Today Magee and Company exports handwoven Irish tweeds of all weights, styles, and colors to clothing designers and manufacturers all over the world, and most of the weaving is now done in centralized factories in the town of Donegal.

During the latter part of the twentieth century, consistent growth in the Irish economy has encouraged awareness of Ireland's material culture, of which handcrafts make an important contribution. It is estimated that currently there are a greater number of people involved in making crafts than at any time in Irish history. Many of them work in studios in remote parts of the country, far from the markets and people who might be interested in their work.

In 1977, Showcase Ireland was started as a craft fair in the Great Hall of the Royal Dublin Society. Its purpose was to provide a place where craftspeople and buyers could meet. The first Showcase Ireland attracted 35 exhibitors; the eighteenth show will exhibit the work of 480 craftspeople to thousands of buyers from all over the world.

Since medieval times, it has been the custom of kings and presidents to commission special gifts to present to the host country on the occasion of a state visit. Our esteemed president, Mary Robinson, has chosen Irish crafts as gifts for heads of state, including Queen Elizabeth II of England, President François Mitterand of France, King Juan Carlos of Spain, and many others.

Finishing a book is rather like saying good-bye to a friend with whom one has shared a journey. East, west, north, and south, in frost, rain, sun, and snow, wherever there were potters, lacemakers, knitters, basketmakers, or weavers, I was there, talking to them, watching them ply their skills, marveling at the fact that so little has changed over the centuries.

To some extent craftspeople are philosophers of a kind. They have made the choice to dance to the tune of their muse, and in doing so have preserved for us to enjoy traditional skills that reach back to the beginning of time and are a tribute to humankind's unfailing ingenuity.

I shall miss their company.

Irish Hands

The title of this book was inspired by a remark made by Evelyn Gleeson, a prominent figure in the Celtic revival in arts and crafts that began in London around 1895. Evelyn lived in Sussex, where her father practiced medicine. She was of Irish extraction and eventually the emotional ties she felt for Ireland could no longer be ignored and she returned to live out her life there. As she explained it to a friend, "I have come back to Ireland to find work for Irish hands in the making of beautiful things."

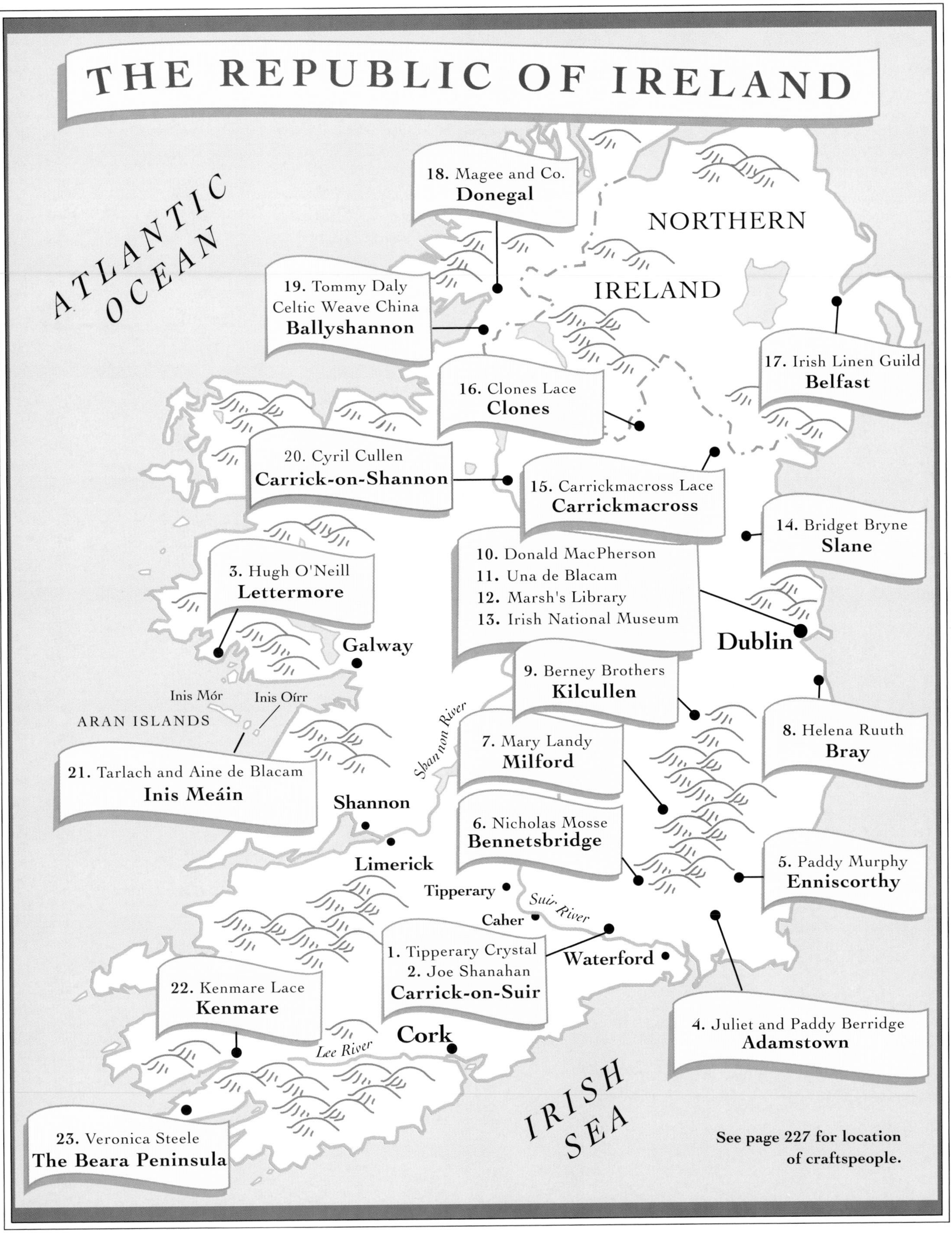

THE REPUBLIC OF IRELAND

ATLANTIC OCEAN

NORTHERN IRELAND

IRISH SEA

18. Magee and Co.
Donegal

19. Tommy Daly
Celtic Weave China
Ballyshannon

17. Irish Linen Guild
Belfast

16. Clones Lace
Clones

20. Cyril Cullen
Carrick-on-Shannon

15. Carrickmacross Lace
Carrickmacross

14. Bridget Bryne
Slane

3. Hugh O'Neill
Lettermore

Galway

10. Donald MacPherson
11. Una de Blacam
12. Marsh's Library
13. Irish National Museum

Dublin

Inis Mór   Inis Oírr

ARAN ISLANDS

9. Berney Brothers
Kilcullen

8. Helena Ruuth
Bray

21. Tarlach and Aine de Blacam
Inis Meáin

Shannon River

7. Mary Landy
Milford

Shannon

6. Nicholas Mosse
Bennetsbridge

5. Paddy Murphy
Enniscorthy

Limerick

Tipperary

Suir River

Caher

1. Tipperary Crystal
2. Joe Shanahan
Carrick-on-Suir

Waterford

22. Kenmare Lace
Kenmare

Lee River

Cork

4. Juliet and Paddy Berridge
Adamstown

23. Veronica Steele
The Beara Peninsula

See page 227 for location of craftspeople.

In and On the
Irish House

Pottery

Glass

Basketmaking and Wickerwork

Thatching

Pottery

Pottery, in its broadest meaning, includes all objects fashioned from clay and then hardened by fire, although there is a growing tendency to restrict the word to the commoner articles of this class, and to apply the word "porcelain" to all finer varieties. The very existence of pottery is dependent on two important natural characteristics in the clay, the ability to be readily kneaded, or

molded, while moist, and the ability to convert from soft clay into almost indestructable objects when fired at appropriate temperatures. The craft of pottery was not

brought down from heaven by one

of the gods to a favorite race,

as the myths of all the earlier

civilizations, Egyptian, Greek,

Scythian, and Chinese, would

have us believe, but born from the brain and hand of

man, struggling to fulfill his allotted task. Since the

middle of the nineteenth century, research has established

beyond doubt that wherever clay was found, men became

potters of a sort, just   as they became hunters,

farmers, carpenters,   and metalworkers, by

sheer force of need   and slowly gathered tra-

dition. Every   small fragment of

locally made   ware is important to

archaeologists.   When reassembled,

Early pot or food vessel, c. 1800 B.C., found in Killinagh, County Cavan, shows a surprising harmony in form and decoration.

their shapes and decorative motifs indicate patterns of social customs, migration, contact, and trade, as well as help date associated finds. For approximately five thousand years, pottery has been part of everyday life in Ireland. Our first ancestors were nomadic figures who arrived so long ago that hardly anything is known about them. They were followed around 5000 B.C. by the first farmers. They probably brought with them seeds of corn, and certainly their farm implements. What they found was a country almost covered with primeval forests of oak, pine, elm, and hazel which harbored grouse, pigeon, and duck, as well as

red deer and wild pig; rivers teeming with salmon, trout, and eel, and bushes laden with fruit. These were the Neolithic people and it was they who introduced pottery to Ireland as well as the crafts of spinning and weaving.

The earliest wares were handmade for the communities' domestic and funerary requirements. Although these were mainly utilitarian, shards recovered by archaeologists show them to have a surprising harmony in form and decoration.

The great revolution in pottery-making was the invention of the wheel; it was arrived at independently by many civilizations. In its most primitive form it can still be seen today in parts of India, Sri Lanka, China, and Japan. In Egypt during the seventeenth century a further advance in its development was made, and this form remains the best and most used for the production of fine pottery.

It was the Anglo-Normans who introduced the wheel into Ireland. Up to this time, for some reason, Ireland retained a rather casual attitude toward developing an indigenous style of pottery. The arrival of the Anglo-Normans changed all that. They had a life-style to maintain; they imported quantities of glazed and decorated pottery from Bristol, Gloucester, and also from Rouen in France, Germany, Spain, and Italy. The expertise required for wheel-turning was quickly learned and soon jugs, cooking pots, lamps, and vessels for washing hands, as well as other items were being made. Some potters specialized in making tiles for roofs and floors. By the early part of the fourteenth century these Irish potters had become quite a force in urban and Anglicized areas.

As always social trends demand change and the removal of the fireplace from the center to the side or end of the room, in the late fifteenth century, created a distinction between dining and cooking areas and consequently a division in styles between utilitarian and decorative tableware.

In the seventeenth century, coffee, tea, and chocolate drinking became the fashion, and the ritual surrounding it created a demand for more elegant tableware. By the late seventeenth century the Irish economy was expanding and the higher standard of living allowed not just the very rich families to indulge in displays of wealth but some of the middle classes as well, increasing the demand for attractive tableware.

A tin-glazed earthenware (or delftware) was developed in Antwerp in the sixteenth century; it was a soft baked clay body covered with tin enamel. Delftware does not appear to have been made in Ireland until 1735. Two plates exist with this date mark, and were probably produced by John Chambers. By far the most important of the delft-makers was Captain Henry Delamain. Delamain was born in County Kildare, but had lived abroad for twenty years where he claimed to have learned the art of manufacturing delft and earthenware.

The Royal Dublin Society, founded in 1731, encouraged high standards in native industry. They were disturbed by the high importation of so much "foreign" pottery into the country. The society gave generous

Irish delftware plate in manganese and white, depicting a landscape, probably painted by Peter Shee. Made in the workshop of Captain Henry Delamain, c. 1745.

financial assistance to fledgling craftspeople. Delamain took up this challenge, and in 1752 took over an already established but unsuccessful pottery. He extended the factory by building kilns and warehouses and he reemployed the more skilled workmen. In time they produced dinner services, spirit barrels, wall-fountains (or cisterns), apothecary jars, and much more. The ware was painted blue and white and also manganese and white. The decoration sometimes copied traditional Chinese motifs, others had views of gentlemen's country seats, with landscapes, coats of arms, or crests. Delamain ware was exported to Germany, Spain, Portugal, and the West Indies. Like other master potters, Henry Delamain spent a lot of his time on scientific experiments. He tried various clays, but in the end remained faithful to the white clay of Carrickfergus. This clay was also exported to competitors in Bristol, Liverpool, and Glasgow.

As far as shapes are concerned, a certain jug, the barrel, and the wall cistern do not appear to have been shapes used outside Ireland.

Toward the end of.the eighteenth century, Irish potters were trying to compete against mass-produced imported ware; the prohibitive cost of coal needed to fire the kilns made for difficulties which eventually became insurmountable, and many small potteries closed down. Henry Delamain died in 1757, but the pottery was carried on by his widow until her death in 1760. War on the Continent stopped the Delamain export trade; it became more difficult for an Irish delftware pottery to compete with huge potteries in Staffordshire, England, and the fine quality of the continental

Rare blue-and-white Irish delftware water cistern, Captain Henry Delamain, c. 1745.

porcelain, and in the end, it too failed.

The demise of the Irish fine-ware potteries coincided with an increase in the number of high-class ceramic retailers. Josiah Wedgwood, because of overproduction at his Etruria factory, would seem to have been the first to open a shop in Dublin, around 1772. His instructions to his Dublin staff were the same as to his employees elsewhere, and that was to cultivate members of the aristocracy as clientele, so as to make the ware fashionable.

A family who learned much from Wedgwood's business attitudes was James Donovan and Son, George's Quay, Dublin. Like Wedgwood, Donovan cultivated an aristocratic clientele, and had a most prestigious Irish sales outlet for ceramics.

The only porcelain factory of any significance in Ireland was that founded at Belleek, County Fermanagh, in about 1847.

The Great Famine in 1846 had a most devastating effect on Ireland, and within a few years, death and emigration, both a result of the famine, had halved the population. Those who were left were greatly impoverished. In 1847 John Caldwell Bloomfield took over his father's estate at Castle Caldwell, and, in order to provide a regular income for his tenants, he set up several ventures, such as lacemaking, embroidery, and the export of porcelain clay. Belleek clay had already been identified as something special and had been used by the Worcester pottery with great success.

Hard-paste porcelain was made at Belleek because of the presence of large deposits of suitable china clay (feldspar and kaolin) on the Castle Caldwell estate. The initiative in starting manufacture was taken by Robert Armstrong, a Dublin architect, then working for W. H. Kerr, one of the proprietors of the Royal Worcester Porcelain factory. Financial support was provided by a Dublin businessman, David McBirney,

and the new works were completed in 1860. The porcelain body was not perfected until 1863 when William Bromley, the foreman of W. H. Goss of Stoke-on-Trent, was employed and brought with him a dozen or so experienced workmen. The nature of early Belleek owed much to the background of these men. To this day, the chief characteristics of Belleek are fine translucency and a warm ivory color.

The era of the studio ceramics began with Frederick Vodrey toward the end of the nineteenth century. He produced fine-quality vases influenced by classical and Japanese forms. It was Vodrey who pioneered the use of Celtic motifs on ceramics.

The introduction of the small electric kiln (the first such reputed to be used in Dublin in 1930) gave freedom to the individual artist-potter. Outstanding among these studio potters in the latter half of the twentieth century were Peter Brennan from 1941, John French from 1950, and Grattan Freyer from 1952; their achievements brought a fresh public interest, and, as a result, the Craft Potters Society of Ireland was established in 1977.

Blue-and-white Irish delftware round platter,
Captain Henry Delamain, c. 1745.

Tommy Daly
Celtic Weave China

Had Tommy Daly been alive at the time European princes patronized the arts, he would surely have received a Royal warrant; most notably from France, where decorative china had reached a high level of design and was much sought after. Marie Antoinette, princes of the blood, and members of the aristocracy (such as the Duc d'Angoulême at rue de Bondy) were actively involved in the design and manufacture of fine china.

The flowering of the decorative arts reached a peak in the eighteenth century. Now, toward the end of the twentieth century, only a select few practice the most delicate, most skilled, and most precise of the craft—the weaving of china baskets and the making of china flowers. Up-to-date methods of pottery production have ensured that certain processes can be partially automated, but each woven basket and

each flower made by Celtic Weave China, even when produced to a common design, has to be individually crafted entirely by hand.

I decide to visit Tommy Daly in his workshop at Cloghore, a small townland on the borders of the counties Donegal and Fermanagh, less than a mile from the village of Belleek.

It is late autumn and the days are becoming shorter, so an early morning start is to be recommended. The night before the journey northward I look at the sky for an indication of tomorrow's weather; dove-gray clouds as tenuous as smoke puffs drift and dissolve against a seemingly limitless flame-colored sky—a sure indication of heavy frost in the morning. But the anticipation of frost makes for no change in plan. Irish people are undeterred

by weather; they will stand all day in drizzling rain, as happily as in the sun.

Northern counties fare less well than their southern neighbors in the quality of their land. In counties Cavan, Monaghan, and Leitrim, farmers have to work hard to make a living from their holdings. But even if the land is not as rich as it might be, or the scenery as lush as in the southeast, or as dramatically beautiful as in the west, these northbound counties have their own quiet charm, not least being the location of several beautiful lakes.

The fog, natural companion of a heavy frost, transformed everything it touched. Lough Sheelin, near Cavan, was covered by a pearly mist; white swans moved like wraiths through the haze which hung low over the water. Occasionally columns of pale autumn sunlight break through and rest on the surface of the lake, twinkling like an array of golden nuggets. Roadside flowers still blossoming in the tangle of brown vegetation are the white trumpets of convolvulus, and an occasional branch of fuchsia, their lanterns of rich scarlet and purple making a bright dash of color against a muted background.

Traffic is light, and before noon I am in the village of Belleek; ten minutes later I reach Tommy Daly's workshop, and am being introduced to his wife, Patricia, who is responsible for painting on the china flowers, and his son, Adrian, who is in charge of production.

Celtic Weave China is a family affair. Tommy's grandfather and his father spent all their working lives at the Belleek Potteries, as did Tommy, until 1982, when he decided to form his own pottery and Celtic Weave China came into being. Adrian,

Tommy's son, had more or less decided to study architecture, when, as a summer job, he went into the pottery's workshop. By the end of six weeks working there he knew, without a shadow of a doubt, that this was the work he wanted to do most, and so became the fourth generation of the Daly family to work at this craft.

Basket- and flower-making were introduced to Ireland about one hundred twenty years ago by a William Henshall from Stoke-on-Trent. Henshall worked with Belleek Pottery from 1863 until 1908 and brought with him a craft which was already being practiced in some potteries in England, most notably Worcester. Some innovative designs were developed in the early 1930s at Belleek, but for the following half century, very few new designs were introduced.

In the early 1930s a skilled potter, Johnny Flynn, established a small pottery called Cloghore Pottery. He produced a few designs of small baskets in the shamrock shape. They were of excellent quality, but due to lack of capital this enterprise failed in 1936, and Johnny returned to work for Belleek Potteries. All that remains of Cloghore Pottery's production is now held in private collections.

As a young man Tommy had become impatient at the lack of new designs which were emerging from Belleek. His ambition was to produce a collection of baskets and floral items which would be unique in both design and material. At his own pottery, he performed many experiments with different components, and trials were undertaken to obtain the optimal match of materials and translucent glaze. The final

Tommy Daly puts the final petal on a china rose and then places the rose on a woven china box. Exclusive to Tiffany & Co.

choice was a carefully balanced mixture of feldspar china clay, bone ash, and very fine gum arabic. The latter produces a beautiful crisp white "body," which allows greater detail in the handcraft of the floral sprays. Firing this material to the appropriate temperature, and for the required duration, gives significant added strength to the finished product, while retaining the original fragile appearance.

The raw material ingredients are mixed in a fashion similar to the kneading of dough in breadmaking, with the mix being left to mature for up to twenty weeks. Air is removed and the texture improved by a beating process using oak hand beaters on an oak block. The material is then fed into a hand-operated extruder which produces continuous spaghettilike strands for weaving.

In making a basket, the base is hand plaited on a ceramic tile with a three-strand plait. (Celtic weavers use a three-strand plait for its basket products in order to give extra fineness and detail.) The open trellis-work is attached by hand to the dried base on a plaster of Paris mold, using only the craftsman's eye to determine shape and angle, and laying each strand individually. Left overnight to dry, the outline of the basket is now formed and the edges are applied, using two strands of material. The edges which will subsequently hold the floral sprays are attached to

the basket using a ropelike roll produced from the strands of extruded clay. Additional features such as handles, legs or stands, as appropriate, are formed by hand, rolling the clay on a workbench and shaping it to the required form. Flowers, stems, buds, and leaves are all individually crafted in the palm of the maker's hand. Some flowers contain as many as sixty individual petals and are built up one by one. One of the flowering tools used by Adrian Daly in the shaping of the petals has been handed down within the family for four generations.

The selected floral display is applied at the appropriate stage in the drying process. The selection of this is of paramount importance, as there is significant contraction during this phase. The basket is now ready for the first or bisque firing, which is fraught with problems as there is a 16 percent contraction or shrinkage in virtually every dimension of the original greenware. Each piece has to be supported during this phase, which lasts for about forty hours, in a very precisely predetermined pattern of heat levels which range to a maximum of 1,260 degrees centigrade. During the firing the material changes from its original dull gray color to a crisp, fine china white.

The basket, or the flower-ware, is now checked after the bisque firing and a specially formulated glaze is applied using an air-spraying

Patricia Daly painting a china flower.

method which allows for an even glaze coating; this produces a high-gloss finish after the item is fired for the second time in a gloss kiln at 1,140 degrees centigrade.

Each piece of Celtic Weave China is hand-painted by Patricia Daly. The colors, in which pastel shades predominate, are carefully selected to highlight the lifelike quality of the floral designs. This is a time-consuming, painstaking process involving deftness and delicacy of touch. After hand-painting, the item is again fired, this time at 820 degrees centigrade.

Having toured the workshop and listened to the description of the processes involved in making such lovely objects, I sat down and watched Tommy, his deft fingers working at lightning speed, make from a ball of clay a glorious assembly of flowers—roses,

carnations, lilies-of-the-valley, morning glories. One can only watch and wonder at such a gift. Even at the height of their success, the china factories in Sèvres, Chantilly, and Vincennes could not have surpassed in beauty the flowers taking shape before me in this workshop in a remote corner of Ireland.

On the journey back to Dublin, my mind

Woven china honeypot is the centerpiece of a breakfast tray.

is occupied with all I have seen and learned at Celtic Weave China. I could visualize the spaghettilike weave used to fashion a heart-shaped box, or a square box with a painted flower on its lid, or  perhaps a honey pot shaped like a beehive —the possibilities are endless and fill me with excited anticipation.

By now all traces of fog have disappeared, and I can appreciate the soft green fields of County Fermanagh and its blue lakes glistening in the sun. There is a nip in the air; I notice a dramatic change in the trees since a week ago. Most have reached their peak and many are already bare. But winter has its own beauty; in its solitude the landscape gives something different and infinitely precious to those who love it. There are certain lighting effects of golden trees against slate-gray skies, or the red stems of the dogwood lit by a single ray of sunset, after weeks of chill fog which goes straight to the heart.

Nicholas Mosse

Nicholas Mosse Pottery

Kilkenny city is one of Ireland's largest craft centers. It is dominated by the spectacular Kilkenny Castle, which dates from 1192, and which overlooks the river Nore.

The city itself is old and retains much of its medieval character. Small wonder then that it is a fertile breeding ground for craftsmen such as Nicholas Mosse, whose pottery, situated in an old mill in Bennettsbridge, is only two miles south of the city. It is in this environment of rural splendor with a view of the river and the city that Mosse creates his celebrated spongeware. Of his life as a potter, Mosse is most enthusiastic and forthcoming.

I was seven years old when I decided that one day I would become a potter. My father, Stanley Mosse, took me along when he was visiting a friend who had a potter's wheel. Restless and bored with the conversation of the adults, it was suggested that I might amuse myself with the potter's wheel and some clay. As soon as I had my hands on the wheel and felt the smooth pliable texture of the clay, I knew that I had found my role in life; I would become a potter. There would be no deviation from that decision, and my formative years were spent working toward that goal.

My school days behind me, I attended classes at the Harrow School of Art in London. The sixties were an exciting time to be involved in the arts and crafts. There was a revival of interest in the handcrafts such as had not been experienced since the days of William Morris. The school specialized in making pots, and training people to make them in quantity. I became known as the student who made the most pots in the shortest time!

After graduation I spent several years as a journeyman potter, working in England, Scotland, and France, and finally Japan for a year. While I was there it was my good fortune to study under the Number Two Potter Master. The influence of that year in Japan on both my work and my life was profound and far-reaching.

My childhood in Ireland had been an idyllic experience. For generations my father's family had been millers. Their mill was on the River Nore, at Bennettsbridge, a small village outside the city of Kilkenny. His personal interests were almost entirely artistic, so it was with some regret that circumstances were such that he had to leave the art school he was attending in England, and return to Ireland to enter the family business. Perhaps it was because of his own lost opportunities that he encouraged his four children in their artistic tendencies.

My only sister became a stone carver, one of my two brothers is a superb wood-turner and the other brother is an artist. Both my mother and father were art collectors and were also very interested in and knowledgeable about Irish culture and folklore. Many of my mother's and father's extensive collection of spongeware was bought for very little money in local farmers' markets, and sometimes even from traveling people. They were instrumental in the formation of the Irish Country Furniture Society, which was founded to protect Irish furniture and other artifacts from total exportation.

With such a background it was not unexpected that I should have inherited a strong sense of tradition and real love of Irish design. I realized that the years of traveling and study had been leading me toward a decision—to return to Ireland and start my own pottery in Bennettsbridge. My father gave me a disused cowshed which I proceeded to convert into a pottery. This, and a bank loan of three thousand, sent me on my way.

By a happy coincidence, around the same time I met the girl who was to become my wife, and

who would also become invaluable to me in my work. Her name is Susan and she is American, from St. Louis.

Susan had come to Ireland in the wake of her mother's death. What she had read about the peace and tranquility of the country seemed to answer a need at that moment in her life. She planned to stay for about four weeks, but she liked what she saw, and decided to lengthen her visit and to open a small restaurant in the west of Ireland. It was her quest for unusual plates for the restaurant which led her to my pottery. Within a year we were married. The year was 1976.

My ambition was to employ in the pottery as many local people as possible and to use Irish clay in a mixture that had not been used hitherto. In the first year I hired a fourteen-year-old local boy, Francis Power, to help in the pottery. Now, fifteen years on, he is a master potter. At the same time another fifteen-year-old boy was hired, and he has since become our senior decorator.

The clay took longer to develop.

The first pieces Nicholas Mosse Pottery produced were a slip-trailed earthenware; unfortunately, they did not sell well enough. Then we began a phase of salt-glazing pottery. The pieces were beautiful, but very expensive to produce, and this had to cease also, when we realized that we were nearly bankrupt. After this we settled into making very strong regular glazed stoneware, decorated with blue sponged cobalt designs. These were heavy, good country pots and lent themselves to lots of kitchenware which my cooking wife, Susan, used to great advantage. We made lots of unusual kitchen implements such as steamers, bread bakers, ham-salting pans, cheese drainers; if we could

Nicholas Mosse throwing a pot on a wheel.

Nicholas Mosse applying Sybil Connolly's Bennettsbridge Pattern
to a bowl exclusive to Tiffany & Co.

Terra-cotta pots ready for firing at Nicholas Mosse Pottery.

use it, we made it! But that was not very profit-
able either.

The family mill became available and I was
able to buy it at a reasonable price. The idea of
working out of the old mill appealed
to me. One of the important
attractions was a disused hy-
droelectric plant; if I could get it
reactivated I could see that it held
potential for the pottery, making
us self-sufficient as far as energy
was concerned. It took two years
to restore the hydro, but it has
been of immense value to the
pottery, supplying cheap power

which is under our own control. The next big
decision was to move the pottery down to the
actual generator. Because earthenware had to be
used to fire the electric kilns, the whole style of
our pottery changed.

For a long time I had been
working on finding an Irish
clay which would be unique to
Nicholas Mosse Pottery. In a
very old treatise on clay I had
read about a deposit which
Wedgwood reputedly used in
the eighteenth century. I
managed to take the odd few
hours off to search for this

deposit, shovel in hand, and eventually found the old clay pit covered in brambles and ivy, and half submerged in water. After many disastrous results testing the clay for use I found that a potter friend, Michael Roche, in Wexford was also testing the same clay. We pooled our resources and developed what is a unique Irish earthenware clay. The clay is 35 million years old, so in itself is venerable.

My mother's extensive collection of sponge-ware proved to be my greatest inspiration. Now our earthenware is decorated with bright-colored sponge designs. It has proved to be very successful and our volume of production has been doubled almost every year since we moved into the mill.

The clay is made in the old pottery, just down the road. It is brought to the mill and is pugged and balled and thrown by the throwers. Then it is turned and handled; after that it is slipped and when sufficiently dry it is put into a biscuit kiln and fired for the first time. At this stage the decorators take over. My wife, Susan, actually makes the sponges and works with the decorators to get the right combination of shapes and colors. The decorators band and sponge and brush and do some wax resist where necessary before they hand it over to the glazers who finish it, stamp it, and put it in one of the six or seven kilns that are in constant use. After we have checked for quality, it is packed and shipped to customers around the world.

Many of the hobbies of my childhood have carried through to my later years. I have always loved to fish at night for eels and it is a pleasure shared now that I have two young sons to accompany me. I hardly dare to hope that one, at least, of my sons will continue in the pottery.

Paddy Murphy
Hillview Potteries

On my way to Enniscorthy to visit Paddy Murphy at his Hillview Potteries, in Carly's Bridge, County Wexford, I lost my way. Stopping the car and rolling down the window, I asked directions from an elderly man, who, from his weatherbeaten complexion, I assumed to be a farmer. Because of its comparatively mild climate, Wexford and its neighboring counties are known as the "Sunny Southeast."

At the mention of Paddy Murphy's name, my informant shook his head, and with a knowing smile said,."Ah yes, one of nature's gentlemen." I was soon to find out that this was so.

Following instructions, I turned right at the crossroads onto a narrow country road which led onward through windings and turnings, ascents and descents, past a small churchyard waist-high in frothy Queen Anne's lace. Caught in the sunlight it awaited the brush of Pissarro. It was May and the flower

of the month, the hawthorn (sensibly called the May flower by country folk), is in full bloom. I had never before seen such a profusion of blossoms; it draped the hedgerows which enclosed the succulent green fields like veils of matrimonial lace, so that the whole countryside looked dressed for a wedding.

Hillview Potteries is situated on a steep hill overlooking a panorama of serene countryside. In the valley below the river Urn winds its way through sun-filled water meadows; the distant hills shimmer and appear to sway as light and cloud flick around them. Paddy Murphy is one of the few remaining traditional potters. We exchange greetings over a welcoming cup of tea, and right away I begin to ask him questions about his life and craft.

I am the fifth generation of my family to be a potter; in fact, my family have some four hundred years of the pottery craft in their blood. My

Paddy Murphy working on his terra-cotta garden pots. The pots are dried before being placed in the kiln.

maternal great-grandfather, Samuel Brinkley, was a Master Potter. He lived to be 105 years old and worked at Carly's Bridge for almost ninety years. I learned the craft from my grandfather, Dick Brinkley. My uncles were the last generation to make buttermilk crocks and other items for the dairy and domestic use. Times change and so do the needs of the people. Today I make garden pots, small and large, plain and decorative; seed pans, bulb bowls, parsley pots, hanging baskets, strawberry pots, patio containers, and much more—all in terra-cotta. The name terra-cotta is derived from the Latin, terra cocta; *it means "baked earth."*

Pointing to a nearby field Paddy continues:

Marl is the local name for the clay we use, and it comes from that field. It used to be dug by laborers in the summer months from a depth of seven to eight feet, but now we have machinery which does this work. The clay is hard and lacks plasticity, so it is sprayed with water. Then it is chopped with small wooden spades to make sure that the water penetrates all of the substance. In the winter the frost breaks down the particles; this helps to increase the clay's pliability. After this process, it is covered with damp sacks and polythene, then left to rest for as long as possible. When ready, the clay is pressed between rollers; air pockets can make a spinning pot wobble on the wheel, so it is important to give the clay strength by compressing it, after this process the clay is ready for use.

As I watch Paddy knead the clay, almost as one would knead dough when making bread, it occurs to me many of the techniques practiced here are the same as those that have been worked for thousands of years, part of a tradition stretching back to

Pottery tools passed down to Paddy Murphy from his grandfather.

the dawn of time, remarkably unchanged in the present. A Bronze Age potter would feel at home at Hillview Potteries.

After kneading, the clay is formed into balls. From experience Paddy can estimate the size of the ball with his eye. Next, the ball of clay is put on the wheel-head; the motor is started, and with damp hands he begins to make a large garden pot. Within twenty seconds the ball of clay is straightened, so that it all spins true. He opens the ball with his thumb and makes the base hole. Then with both hands he pulls up the walls and shapes the top of the pot. It is only one minute and thirty seconds since Paddy started the pot, and now it is ready for finishing. The walls are smoothed, and the base neatened with the help of a rib. In reply to my question, Paddy says:

Sometimes I use small cogwheels to make bands of impressed decoration, as they used combs and string in early times. Finally, with my fingers I make small "lips" around the rim; this too, is an ancient form of decoration.

After five minutes and thirty seconds the pot is ready to go to the drying shed; here,

Pots being stacked in
the kiln for firing.

row after row of pots await their turn to be fitted into the kiln. Paddy explains:

The process of drying needs constant monitoring. It is important to have free circulation of air at all times in this shed. The pots must be turned regularly, because should they dry unevenly, or too quickly, it might result in the appearance of cracks. It takes five or six weeks for the pots to be dry enough for firing.

The kiln is a curved beehive type, built from bricks. It can hold up to twenty thousand pots of varying size. The largest pots go at the top because this is where the heat is at its most fierce.

The pots are stacked upside down and one on top of another. It takes two days to fill the kiln. Starting on Monday, it is ready by Wednesday morning to have the coal in the fireholes around the kiln set alight.

The person in charge of the kiln must be careful that the heat builds up slowly and evenly. By Friday the kiln will have burned three to four tons of coal. A check is made that the correct temperature (about 1,200 degrees centigrade) has been reached, then

Derek O'Rourke, Paddy's nephew, throwing a pot.

slowly the fires are allowed to go out, and the kiln is allowed to cool down. Several days later the kiln is emptied of the finished terra-cotta pots.

A love of pottery permeates Paddy Murphy's life. He feels a link with potters past and present.

"In this computer age, I like the idea of being able to use a raw material as basic and humble as clay and make a living out of it."

Derek O'Rourke, Paddy's eleven-year-old nephew, spends all his free time at the pottery. On the day I visited there he had taken a day off school in order to show me his skills at throwing a pot. His obvious love of the potteries ensures the continuation of this tradition for at least another generation.

When Paddy Murphy is not potting, he is either gardening or fishing. He has fished the Urn river since childhood; he maintains that nature is both his inspiration and his education. He bemoans the fact that the fields around his home no longer resound with the symphony of birdsong he had

known in his youth. There are few cuckoos
nowadays, and he has forgotten what it
was like to hear the cry of the corncrake in
the hayfields. He blames the rise in intensive farming and the consequent removal
of hedgerows for the loss of the birdsong
which evoked his childhood and a simpler
rural past.

Despite these regrets, it would be hard to
find a more content man than Paddy Murphy. Within a radius of half a mile he has
all he needs for both his work and his re-
laxation.

Glass

When the Celts arrived in Ireland around 500 B.C., among other things they brought with them an ability to work in metal and a distinctive artistic style. Ireland was rich in gold and copper but poor in precious stones.

In order to  highlight the metal objects which they made, the Celts used the millefiori method of infusing glass rods to make jewellike insets and glass beads, the latter probably for personal adornment. Archaeologists have discovered pieces of colored glass at Carranes in County Cork, which suggests that millefiori glass was being produced in Ireland as early as A.D. 600.

When, in the seventh and eighth centuries, Europe was experiencing a cultural eclipse, because of the Barbarians who had conquered the Roman Empire, Ireland's remote position on the periphery of Europe proved to be its protection. The Irish people lived in peace, and the arts flourished in an

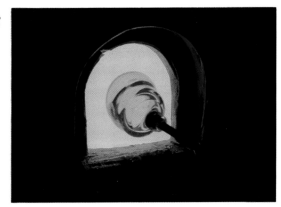

atmosphere conducive to creation. In the ninth century, Ireland's conversion to Christianity inspired her craftsmen to make some of the most perfect objects of that, or any subsequent, age. Pieces such as the Cross of Cong, the Ardagh Chalice, and the Tara Brooch are recognized by art experts the world over as being of exceptional quality. In each of these artifacts the intricate Celtic metalwork is sometimes highlighted by insets of colored glass.

Sybil Connolly's Trellis Pattern, mouth-blown and hand-cut
by Tipperary Crystal. The design is exclusive to
Tiffany & Co.

The earliest record of glassmaking in Ireland dates back to 1258, to William the Glassmaker who most certainly came from Normandy in the wake of the Norman conquest of England. So it was the Normans who first brought glassmaking to Ireland as an industry rather than an art.

In the sixteenth and seventeenth centuries, Venice was the city–state best known for its glassmaking. Their exquisite soda glass was the envy of every European country. Many of the skilled Venetian glassmakers set up plants elsewhere in Europe. One of them, Jacob Verzellini, was working in the North Sea port of Antwerp when his glass was brought to the attention of England's Queen Elizabeth I. In 1571 that enterprising Queen granted him the first patent to make glass in England, and a second, in 1575, to set up a glasshouse in Ireland. A few years later, an Englishman, George Longe, also obtained a patent and he set up his glasshouse about 1590 in what is still known as Curryglass, near Dungarvan, where today Waterford Crystal has its second factory.

Wood was used to stoke the furnaces in the glasshouses. In 1675 restrictions were imposed on the use of wood for such purposes, because as a maritime nation, England was constantly in need of good timber for ships to add to her merchant fleet and the Royal Navy. This imposition was a blow to the glasshouses, but a challenge can make for innovation; that same year an Englishman, George Ravenscroft, found that the introduction of lead oxide (flint) as an ingredient for the raw materials used in glassmaking produced a more durable, heavy, brilliant crystal glass, which was both easier to shape and softer, benefiting both the cutter and the engraver. This innovation would ultimately have a major impact on glassmaking in Ireland.

In 1780 an Anglo-Irish family named Penrose opened a glasshouse in Waterford under the name of the Waterford Flint Glass Warehouse. There are records of the Penrose plant being visited by many distinguished and aristocratic figures of the day. The glass that was produced there reached such a standard of excellence that it be-

came famous on both sides of the Atlantic. Connoisseurs accorded high praise to Penrose glass, and exports flourished. Unfortunately, in the early nineteenth century free trade was abolished and that, with the imposition of heavy taxation, finally forced the closure of the glasshouses in 1851. However, the reputation Penrose Glass had achieved through the excellence of their product was not forgotten; one hundred years later, in 1951, a group of Irish businessmen relit the furnaces, which was to be the beginning of Waterford Crystal.

As a sign of the success of the Waterford revival, a number of glass factories, small and large, have set up around Ireland: Tipperary, Cavan, Galway, and Tyrone, to name just a few. Most of the smaller factories import the blanks for cutting and engraving; Tipperary does not. Every stage of the glassmaking from beginning to end, is carried out on their site at Ballynoran, near Carrick-on-Suir, in County Tipperary. Simon Pearce of Kilkenny, who studied at Venice, and with Orrefors in Sweden, pioneered modern studio glass on his own. He now lives and works in Vermont, and the vacuum he left behind is slowly being filled by other individual glassblowers, such as Keith Ledbetter of Stoneyford, County Kilkenny. Paschal Fitzpatrick specializes in decorative glass at the Craft Centre in Strokestown, County Roscommon.

Tipperary
Crystal

Ray Stafford
Tipperary Crystal

There are few greater satisfactions than to be in the Irish countryside on what the locals refer to as a "pet" day. These days usually occur in early spring when the climate has barely shrugged off the shackles of winter. On such a day I am on the road to visit the plant of Tipperary Crystal.

With admirable foresight, the founders of this crystal company decided to build their glassblowing operation on a thirteen-acre site of outstanding beauty near the border that divides Waterford and Tipperary. Pale golden sunshine highlights the early green leaves on the hedgerows; trees and bushes are full of young birds and their anxious parents. After the somnolence of winter, there are clear signs of awakening, silver catkins glitter on the twigs of the male sallow, and on some bushes the hairy female flowers are already open. The first warblers are arriving, they sing in the translucent green tops of the beeches with a shrill call, and an occasional trill, like a nightingale.

Intensive farming has deci-

mated many of Europe's traditional hay meadows, destroying the matchless intimacy of the countryside, and its variety as well. In the main, Ireland has escaped this calamity. The hedgerows are one of the country's most characteristic features; its patchwork of small fields separated by thick hedges is home to countless indigenous plants and animals, woven into our national folklore and literature. It would be catastrophic to evict them from their ancient habitats. Many naturalists believe that some of the hedgerows now standing were carved from Ireland's original wildwood to act as prehistoric edge markers, others, to act as boundaries for early villages; their location and composition have much to tell us about the lives of our ancestors.

The comparative peace of the Irish roads allows me to muse. With my destination in mind, it occurs to me that it seems almost inappropriate that a small, mainly agricultural country like Ireland, so remotely situated on the

western edge of Europe, should lay claim to the biggest craft industry in the world; but the making of full lead crystal is, in fact, just that.

The formation of Tipperary Crystal coincided with a reduction in staff at Waterford Crystal, thereby presenting Tipperary with a wonderful opportunity—a trained and highly skilled workforce on their doorstep.

Most of these workers joined Waterford Crystal as soon as they were old enough to leave school; the invitation to join Tipperary glassworks at that opportune moment meant that the years spent perfecting their skills would not be wasted. This also influenced the development of a thirteen-acre site near the border dividing Tipperary and Waterford, making it easy for the workforce to get to their jobs.

When I arrive at my destination, I am met by Ray Stafford, a tall, personable man in his mid-forties who had already established himself as a successful businessman when he took over Tipperary Crystal. At that time the crystal company employed

thirty people; now, a few years on, its workforce numbers ninety. There are no long-term plans to exceed this figure; quality control is high on Ray's list of priorities. He feels the best way to maintain this is to limit the firm's expansion. In other words, for Tipperary, "small is beautiful."

We begin a tour of the workshop with Ray explaining the skills involved; the manufacture of fine, handmade crystal is both an art and a science, requiring years of dedicated skill and meticulous care. The initial apprenticeship is five years, with an additional seven years to become a master craftsman. Even so, every new design presents a challenge to the workers.

The art of glassmaking has hardly changed in two hundred years. The ingredients are potash, ultra-silica sand, and powdery red oxide. These are mixed with cullet (discarded slivers of broken crystal). When heated the cullet melts first, helping the other chemicals to fuse. The "lump" or "gather" of molten glass comes out of the furnace at the end of the blowing iron (a

Gathering, the process of placing molten glass on a rod, is the first step in glassblowing.

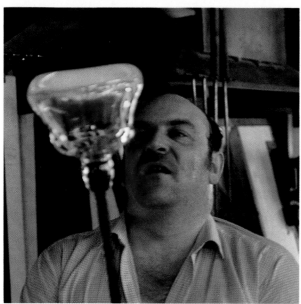

Shaping the molten glass.

hollow metal tube), on its way to be shaped, blown, and molded.

The blower controls the compressed air inside the molten glass. The blowing iron is steadied on a rest, and the molten stem of the glass is added to the body.

The completed piece must pass through a large annealing oven which brings the crys-

Master cutter grinding a pattern into a glass bowl.

tal close to melting temperature and releases the inner tensions so that the parts fuse, guaranteeing perfectly married joints. With expert precision, the master cuts on the black lines that have been put on the blank crystal to indicate where the cuts are to be made.

There is a vaguely mysterious quality about glass-blowing, something almost medieval; so few of the practices have changed over hundreds of years. Perhaps the biggest change is that in the old days the furnaces were stoked with wood; today, they are generated by gas.

Tipperary Crystal is totally self-contained. No glass shapes are imported for cutting—

every item of glass is mouth blown and hand cut on the premises. Reputedly there are just six glass houses in the world today who follow this practice entirely.

In the first few years of its existence, the domestic market bought all the crystal Tipperary could produce; then, through a chance meeting, John Loring, senior vice-president and design director of Tiffany & Company of New York, visited the plant and showed a positive interest in its development. Now, several years later, exclusive cuttings designed for Tiffany's have enjoyed a high level of success.

I am struck by the happy atmosphere generated by the workforce. Everyone seems to like what they are doing, and yet, when interrupted in their task to answer a question about their work, they are unfailingly polite and eager to show their skills. Undoubtedly Ray Stafford has infected them with his enthusiasm for their craft. He is a man with a mission, which is to make Tipperary Crystal famous around the world for its quality and design.

Before I leave, I am proudly shown photographs of Pope John Paul II, President George Bush, and Mikhail Gorbachev, all of whom display pieces of Tipperary Crystal in their respective offices. There is no doubt that in a comparatively short space of time, this glasshouse has made remarkable inroads into the market.

I take leave of Ray, and cross the road to where a ruin of a castle serves as a solid reminder of the arrival of the Normans in 1171. All over Ireland countless such ruins stand open to the sky; after nine hundred years it is usually just the keep that has survived. Ivy almost obscures the ancient stone walls; birds build their nests in the crevices and fly complacently in and out of the slits that serve as windows. A few yards away the River Suir, looking like a silver ribbon in the fading sunlight, flows peacefully along the valley. A sudden breeze sends ripples through the tall river grasses, a reminder that the year is still young. If I am to be home before dark, I must be on my way.

Basketmaking and Wickerwork

Basketmaking is the oldest craft of all, taking precedence even over pottery. A basket is a vessel made of twigs, willow,  or rushes, as well as a variety of other materials, interwoven together, and used for holding, protecting, or carrying any commodity. The process of interweaving twigs, rushes, or leaves is one of the most universal of crafts. It also ranks among the most ancient, probably being the origin of all the textile arts. Decorative designs on old ceramic ware are derived from the marks left from the basket mold used before the invention of the potter's wheel. In the willow pattern on old china, and also on the capitals and moldings of Byzantine architecture, the influence of the basketmaker's art is clearly traceable. Essentially a primitive craft, its relative importance is in inverse ratio to the industrial development of a  people. Among many cultures, baskets of superior quality are made and applied to various useful purposes. North American Indians prepare strong watertight baskets from the roots of a species of abies, which are frequently adorned with decorative patterns made from the dyed quills of the indigenous porcupine. South Africans are similarly skilled in using the ilala reed and the roots of plants, while the Abyssinians and the tribes of central Africa display great adroitness in the art of basket weaving.

No machinery is used in basketmaking. Considerable training and natural aptitude are required. The ultimate perfection of shape and beauty of texture depends upon the more or less perfect conception of form in the craftsman's mind and on his power to impress it on a recalcitrant material.

The materials actually employed in the construction of baskets are numerous and varied, but it is from certain species of willow that the largest supply of basket-making materials is produced. Willows are roughly classed by the basketmaker into "osier" and "fine." The former consists of varieties of the true osier, *Salix viminalis,* the latter, of varieties of *Salix triandra, S. purpurea,* and some other species of hybrids of tougher texture. For the coarser work, dried unpeeled osiers, known as brown stuff, are used; for finer work white (peeled) stuff, and buff (willow stained a tawny hue by boiling them previous to peeling).

The tools required by a willow basket-maker are few and simple. They consist of a sharp knife for cutting out materials, a picking knife for cutting off the protruding butts and tops of the rods after the work is completed, two or three bodkins of varying sizes, a flat piece of iron somewhat narrowly triangular in shape for driving the work closely together, a stout pair of shears and a "dod" or "commander" for straightening sticks. Sometimes there is a screw block or vise for gripping the bottom and cover sticks of a square work, and a lap-board upon which the basketmaker fixes the upsetted bottom while sliding up the basket.

Basketmaking, however, has by no means been confined to the fabrication of those simple and useful utensils from which its name is derived. Of old, the shields of soldiers were fashioned of wickerwork, either plain or covered with hides. The huts of the earliest settlers in Rome, and in Western Europe generally, were made of osier work plastered with clay. Boats of the same material covered with animal skins were used in Britain at the time of the Roman invasion. Nor have the methods much changed. The strokes employed in the construction of basketwork found in Etruscan tombs and now exhibited in the Museo Etrusco at Florence, and in similar articles discovered in Egyptian tombs, are the same as those used by the Irish basketmaker today.

Because of the nature of the materials used, early examples of the craft in a good state of preservation are few. However, the bogs in counties Tipperary and Westmeath have yielded some remnants that have been reliably dated to Neolithic times. Evidence of basket-wickerwork in many of the crannogs or lake dwellings of Ireland date from late Bronze Age to early Christian times. The Ballinderry crannog in County Offaly revealed a number of small wicker huts dated between the fourth and first centuries B.C. It is possible that the walls of the huts were smeared with clay, and that the roofs were thatched. Excavations in Dublin revealed evidence of the use of wickerwork as dividing fences between plots, walls of houses, marking off areas (perhaps for sleeping) within houses, and floor mats. The materials used were willow, hazel, and silver birch. Willow and osier were by far the most common materials

used, and it is so today. There are sixty varieties recorded in Ireland, alone. Willow grows quickly, needs little attention, and very few tools are needed because the rods are pliable, enabling the worker to fashion it to a shape of his choice. Included in the species are any of the trees in the genus *Salix*. It is supposed that from this comes the name "sally" by which the material used by these craftspeople is referred. Willow plots were known as sally gardens, and at one time they were as common a feature of rural Ireland as the potato plot.

Basketmaking in Ireland was a traditional hearth industry. However, in the depressed financial climate of the early part of this century, a workingman, James Holland, set up a small factory for making baskets at Aghagallon, near the banks of Lough Neagh in the southwest corner of County Antrim. For as long as anyone could remember, osier culture and the related craft of making baskets had been practiced in that area. Proximity of willow rods growing in Lough Neagh, and the poverty of the people, made the use of every available natural source a necessity. They made lobster creels, eel traps, and turf baskets

shaped like panniers to load onto the donkey's back for transporting the peat from the bogs where it had been harvested, but by far the majority of baskets made were potato baskets.

The traditional potato basket was a thing of beauty, well designed and beautifully made. The high-quality material from which it was constructed meant that it lasted for years, despite the rough treatment it received, thrown down in muddy potato fields, pushed around by hobnailed boots, and banged off the wooden sides of farm carts. A good basketmaker made about ten baskets a day. They received five shillings and sixpence a dozen for these and they could make about four and a half dozen in a five-and-a-half-day week.

New designs such as cachepots to hold potted plants, baskets that are, in fact, more like summer handbags, tissue containers, all made in beautiful Lake Sedge, are being introduced as additions to the classic shapes, so, perhaps, as people become tired of plastic bags which litter the environment, we will see a strong revival in Ireland of this most ancient craft.

Mary Landy
Basketmaker

While researching this book, I asked the Keeper of Antiquities at the National Museum in Dublin how he would differentiate between art and craft; he considered the question, and then admitted the answer to be a most tantalizing dilemma.

Distinction between the two has never been more blurred. Traditional potters, wood-carvers, and basket weavers behave very much like artists; they all manipulate things individually by hand, and share a creative impulse. One difference is that craft does not have to carry great messages, and unlike artists, craftspeople see themselves as running businesses. In any case, there has been and always will be a handful of craftsmen, painters, or sculptors, who will produce work of quality of expression that goes beyond the ordinary.

Mary Landy is one of these people.

It has been more than twenty years since I first saw Mary Landy demonstrating her skills as a basketmaker in the great hall of the Royal Dublin

Society, Ballsbridge, during the week of the Spring Agricultural Show. A tall, handsome woman, she was weaving rushes into the most beautiful baskets I have ever seen. There was an air of quiet dedication in the manner in which she applied herself to the task. At the end of the demonstration I spoke to her and asked for her name and address, determined to meet her at some future date when she was less occupied.

Several months later I was in the pretty sitting room of her home in Ballinabranna, County Carlow, and in answer to my questions, she told me about her life and her participation in Irish craftwork.

Mary and her twin sister, Brigid, grew up in a household where crafts, such as hand crocheted lace, embroidery, and other forms of needlework, were practiced as naturally as breathing and sleeping. Television, the great distractor, had not as yet penetrated every home in the countryside; people made their own pastimes and amusements. When Mary married Bernard

Landy and came to live in Ballinabranna, she joined the local guild of the Irish Countrywomen's Association (the I.C.A.), which among other functions encouraged the preservation of the indigenous crafts of Ireland. Although a skilled needlewoman, Mary had never worked with rushes, and came to it almost by accident. She had admired rushwork over the years, but had never thought of it as something for her to do.

Then, part of an I.C.A. course in which she participated included rushwork, as well as other crafts. At the culmination of these courses the best pieces of work done in each category were chosen for exhibition at the Dublin Horse Show and also at the Royal Dublin Society of National Crafts competition. Every year from 1972 to 1982 Mary won first prize for her rushwork at the latter exhibition. However, her most prestigious trophy is the highly esteemed and much coveted California Gold Medal which she won in 1982. This was the first time, and so far remains the only time, that the medal was awarded to a work of craft rather than to a work of art. Like the Keeper of Antiquities at the Museum, faced with the quality of Mary Landy's craftwork, the judges had the enterprise and courage to pay her interpretation its rightful tribute.

I asked her to tell me in detail about the rush basketware.

The lake sedge (Scirpus lacustris), *which is found on the margins of some lakes and rivers, is the material used for rush basketwork. It grows up to ten feet high and has thick cylindrical stems. The best rushes grow in deep water and should be cut as near the root as possible. The time to cut is toward the end of July or early August.*

Mary Landy working on rush baskets.

The variety of colors and weave of rushwork.

The rushes must be dried away from direct sunlight and must be turned constantly. When dry, they are tied in bundles and stored standing on their butt ends in a cool shed away from strong light. They are ready for use when they bend without cracking.

Basketmaking is all about control rather than strength. The preparation for working the rushes is important and gives me control. Having the rushes in perfect working condition is obviously of immense importance, and this is one of the drawbacks in attracting people to practice this particular craft. If one soaks the rushes overnight, intending to use them the fol-

lowing day, and then circumstances occur which prevent you from doing so, one has to start all over again, preparing the rushes for use, unlike crochet or needlework, to mention just two of the crafts which one can pick up and work at whenever one finds a free moment. In damp weather the rushes are dipped in water, and rolled in an old blanket for twenty-four hours to soften. In dry weather the rushes are soaked for only twenty minutes. It is also a good idea to wash the rushes before working, using a little soap. Oversoaked, the rushes become pulpy; the perfect condition is when they feel and work like velvet ribbon. It is best not to work in a dry atmosphere—a warm room, a sunny, windy day out-of-doors, or an east wind, as these will quickly turn the rushes dry and brittle.

When asked about the tools needed for the rushwork, she laughs and replies: ''Almost everyone has their own pet tools. When we were learning to do the rushwork, the tools listed were a knife, scissors, packing needle, hammer, tacks, a saddler's palm for heavy work, soft thread and twine for stitching.''

Before I leave, Mary shows me the basket which won her the gold medal. Admiring the quality of her work, it occurred to me that here was the answer to a question concerning me for weeks past—what to give as a housewarming present to someone who had taken up residence in a beautiful late-seventeenth-century château in France, and whose taste in all things epitomizes elegance; in this instance, the French couturier, Hubert de Givenchy. When I suggested to Mary that she might consider weaving the beautiful rushes into baskets to hold tissues, she liked the idea. Now these Irish baskets take pride of place in all three of Givenchy's homes. They have, for me, become the perfect present—a handmade gift from Ireland.

Emerging from the subdued light of indoors, I am struck by the clarity of the light outside; no pollution here! On an impulse I decide to return to Dublin via the network of narrow country roads (called boreens in Ireland) which run almost parallel with the main highway. Motorists still share these secondary roads with roosters, donkeys, even cows if it is near milking time, and the odd goat, so speeding is out of the question which is just as well, as meandering at a slow pace gives one time to enjoy the serenity of the countryside. It is midsummer and nature is at its most bountiful. No intensive farming has so far reached this part of Ireland. On went the hedgerows for hundreds of yards, miles even, down both sides of the boreen, a mass of tangled impregnable vegetation.

Blackberry blossoms were everywhere, as were roses, daisies, and columbines; there were nettles, spider webs, and butterflies. If you shut your eyes and listened, you could hear the bees hovering as they decided which flower to attack, and birds chattering to each other, and sudden skittering noises which could have been field mice. But almost more exciting than anything else was to see wild foxgloves. In my childhood no country walk was complete until you had put fox thimbles on your fingers. It was wonderful to see this hedgerow still existing unspoiled, looking exactly as it must have a hundred years ago. Hedgerows are a living proof that nature is a web of connected activities.

The villages on these quiet roads give much pleasure. Nothing has been prettified, everything is unaffected, simple, honest, and attractive. The pastel painted doorways on the main street—often the only street—remind me of a parade of ice cream lollipops. Adults and children wave as I pass. Memories of such days stay forever in one's mind.

Bridget Byrne
Basketmaker

Bridget Byrne lives with her husband, Martin, on a small farm near the village of Slane, County Meath. The river Boyne flows beside the village and through the surrounding valley; it is one of the rivers in Ireland where the rushes used for basketmaking grow in abundance.

Bridget's son, Frank, is currently working on a commission to replace the rush seats on the hundred-year-old chairs from the interior of Christ Church Cathedral in Dublin, a project that involves a huge quantity of material. When I learned that on a certain Saturday in August he would be cutting rushes in the river, at a point about a mile beyond the village of Slane, I knew that this was a scene for David Davison, the photographer of this book, to record. At an arranged time and place we met Bridget who was accompanied by her eleven-year-old granddaughter, Mary O'Rourke.

The riverside path was narrow, so we parked the car about a mile from our destination, and walked, two by

two, Bridget and her granddaughter leading the way. The signs of autumn were already visible: as Keats called it the "season of mists and mellow fruitfulness." The first blackberries were ripening on the brambles, there was shining black fruit on the elder bushes, and on many hawthorns the abundant berries had already turned crimson. On the embankment Michaelmas daisies and goldenrod that escaped from gardens are coming into bloom. Field bindweed, the wild convolvulus, is everywhere; sometimes it covers a whole hedgebank, like an orchestra of small white trumpets. Somewhere a bird is singing; Bridget identified it as the song of the robin, explaining that this is probably their first autumn song, since they are now taking up their winter territories and they sing to drive off rivals.

Eventually we came to the spot on the river where Frank, with the aid of his young redheaded helper, is cutting the rushes with a sickle. When a decent number has

Frank Byrne harvesting and gathering the rushes in the river Boyne.

River rushes drying against a wall.

been accumulated he wades toward the bank where, watched by a few cows that peer sleepily at us from the opposite side, we all help to arrange the rushes into bundles. Frank has brought along a narrow vehicle, rather like a horse box, that enables the rushes to travel upright. When they are cut they are a strong shade of green. If the weather is dry they will be left outdoors for a few weeks, propped up against a wall of an outbuilding on the Byrnes's farm. Afterward they will be stored in a loft and allowed to dry out even further. The color will gradually change to the distinctive green-beige color that is one of the hallmarks of these Irish rushes.

After our adventures on the riverbank, Bridget takes us to her home for tea; we talk about her life and her involvement with rushes and basketmaking. She was born on a small farm in County Mayo, in the west of Ireland, where the quality of the land, for farming purposes, is notoriously poor; so it comes as no surprise to learn that in her childhood money was in short supply. Nevertheless theirs was a happy household. Circumstances were such that her family had to utilize to their advantage every possible source that nature provided, which was how Bridget, as a young girl, became interested in basketry. Her grandfather, who lived with the family, was a powerful influence on her.

When she was old enough, Bridget would help him harvest the first year's growth of not just willow but all the bounty of the hedgerows: blackberry, snowberry, dogwood, to name just a few. In the winter she would sit in the corner by the fire and watch her grandfather weaving the materials which would provide a new

thatch for the roof of their farmhouse, or filling orders for lobster creels, eel traps, and donkey baskets, and, of course, the different versions of the potato basket. The staple diet of potatoes was steamed in the baskets, and when the family had eaten their fill, whatever was left over was fed to the chickens and other farm animals. All these items made from rushes had Gaelic names and to make it even more complicated, different areas of the country had different names by which to identify the types of baskets.

When Bridget married she moved to Slane, County Meath. The land in Meath is of top quality, and she and her husband settled down happily on their farm to raise a family of seven children. From the riches of the land and the hard work of the parents, all seven children have gone out into the world with a good education and are living successful and happy lives. With her

children provided for, Bridget now had time to become involved with craftwork again.

It was fortunate that An Grianan (translated, it means "The Sunny Place"), an adult education college, whose role is to foster and teach the traditional crafts of Ireland, was situated just a few miles from her home in Slane. At first she entered every competition in order to bring her standard of work up to date. That was twenty years ago. Now she teaches rushwork at An Grianan, and gives demonstrations of basketmaking all over the country.

Her granddaughter, Mary O'Rourke, was taught how to work the rushes as soon as she was old enough to hold the tools. "Whatever else she may learn in her life, she will always have the knowledge of rushwork as a security in times of recession," says her grandmother. Words of wisdom, indeed!

Joe Shanahan
Basketmaker

On my way to visit Joe Shanahan, a willow craftsman of some repute, in Carrick-on-Suir, County Tipperary, a light frost has touched the landscape, etching it with silver. There is excitement in driving through a countryside transformed into a sugared paradise. It is January, the winter so far has been exceptionally mild; even so, when, at the edge of the town of Carrick, I stopped to ask directions, I am mildly surprised to see a cluster of snowdrops at the base of an old oak tree. Some were fully in bloom, others were pushing up a pair of sea-green leaves. Looking more closely, I noticed that among the snowdrops the winter aconites were uncurling and would soon be in flower with a delicate ruff under their butter-yellow petals. Snowdrops and aconites signal the rebirth of the floral year. When I arrive at the workshop, Joe Shanahan, a man of few words, is sitting on a low stool, with his back against the wall, weaving willow rods into baskets of all shapes and sizes. Finished baskets hang

from the ceiling and cover the floor of the large garage-type room which is his workshop. He takes a long time to formulate replies to my questions about his family and his work. Joe pondered each question, but the answers, when they finally came, were considered and precise. He is the third generation of his family to be involved in the weaving of willows, so his knowledge of the craft is extensive.

Basketmaking as a traditional craft has been identified in particular with two areas in Ireland—the shores of Lough Neagh in the southwest corner of County Antrim, in the north of Ireland, and the Suir valley, in the south.

Whereas down through the centuries the majority of baskets were made by people for their own use, basketmaking was also a specialized craft. There were many itinerant basketmakers who traveled around the country offering their services in exchange for a small fee. As with all good craftsmen, top-trade basketmakers were protective, and even secretive,

about the finer points of their work. They preferred to work in private until the basket was almost complete, at which time they were quite pleased to have an audience.

My grandfather, John Shanahan, was apprenticed to a basketmaker in Carrick-on-Suir in 1888. He began by making the potato basket in its many variations. He was ambitious, and good at selling his skills. He soon became the supplier of hampers to British Rail for transporting fowl. He died in 1916; his two sons, Edward, my father, and Michael, carried on the business. The contract with British Rail expired in 1922, but in its place came a contract for

Joe Shanahan weaving large willow peat baskets.

making yeast baskets for transporting yeast from the Watercourse Distillery in Cork to bakers around the countryside.

The overall economic situation was bad in Ireland in the twenties. However, during the Second World War a scarcity of containers kept our workshop fully occupied with orders. During the war the baskets were used for dropping supplies behind enemy lines. My father kept about thirty people fully employed in making willow baskets of different varieties. After the war, baskets were still being used for many purposes; one would see them at railway stations and laundries, for instance. Hurdles for sporting events were another steady source of income.

Since the willows grow beside the river Suir, from which the town of Carrick gets its name, our materials are readily available. It is not a difficult crop to grow, it needs little attention other than careful and frequent weeding during the first two seasons, and annual cutting of the more tender shoots to promote fresh growth. Some species can grow up to twenty feet in two years. In July, willow can grow by as much as two inches per day. You can almost see it growing.

Harvesting occurs annually, and in Ireland the ideal cutting time is between November and February. If left any later than this the sap will have risen in the rods, rendering them less easy to work. In the past, school holidays were usually geared to the willow harvest, even though the harvesting of willow was left to women who had the patience and experience, gleaned over the years, of grading the willow rods. This was of great importance to the basketmaker. When harvested, the rods are tied in bundles and left to dry in a safe place until spring. They are then put standing upright in a stream for several weeks, after which they are removed and peeled with an iron stripper.

In the late fifties and early sixties, everything changed. People started to use plastic containers and the demand for baskets almost ceased. Had we not started to make wicker furniture, which was well received, I doubt that we would have survived.

*Willow reeds for
Joe Shanahan's baskets.*

Joe agrees with me that the wheel is turning, and fashion tinged with ecology has decreed that containers made from natural materials are in demand once more. Both in England and Ireland there is a renewed interest in items made from willow and rushes.

All the time Joe has been talking to me he has continued with his work. A small bundle of willow is woven through the struts which are held in place on a jog; it all looks like a difficult version of knitting to my inexperienced eye.

Thatching

To many people the whitewashed cottage with its thatched roof is an integral part of rural Ireland. It is true that these  cottages nestle into the green fields, hills, and mountains in a way that no other building does. Yet, like so many other crafts, thatching came about through necessity rather than choice. Until the turn of the century, efficient rail and road transport did not exist as it does today, so houses were built using local materials. Slates and tiles have been used in Ireland since the Middle Ages, but only in areas where suitable material could be locally quarried, as in counties Clare, Cork, and Donegal. There was a time

when large woodlands provided abundant timber for all

purposes and then some roofs were covered with shingles —

flat plates of split timber — but in the seventeenth and

eighteenth centuries the destruction of the woods took place

and this particular craft died out. The other and more

common type of roof in most parts of rural Ireland is the

thatched roof. Thatching, which refers to any roof made

of organic material, is the oldest form of roof covering.

In Ireland it dates back at least five thousand years,

and possibly to prehistoric times.

It is a craft which owes

nothing to machinery; indeed

the tools used by today's

thatchers are virtually the

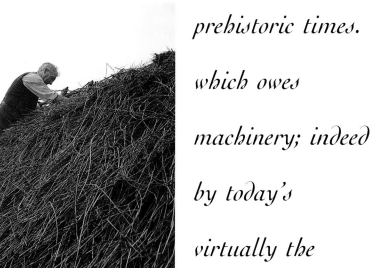

Reconstruction of a Bronze Age village with thatch-roofed dwellings at Craggaunowen, County Clare.

same as those used by their forebears. The materials used for thatching vary from region to region, again relying on what is locally available. Wheat straw, found in most parts of the country, is most commonly used. In northern areas—Derry, Antrim, Fermanagh, and Tyrone—flax is preferred to wheat, because so much flax is grown in Northern Ireland to meet the demands of the Irish linen industry. In mountainous districts, especially in Donegal, Galway, and Kerry, rushes and certain tough grasses are favored.

The floor plan of Irish traditional houses is usually rectangular, consequently the roofs are of simple construction—hip roofs or gable roofs. In northern counties and southwest Munster the gable roof predominates, while in the southeastern counties the hip roof is more commonly used. A thatcher is judged by his ridge as it is the spine so to speak of the roof. As with all things worked by human hand no two roofs are the same; ten identical houses thatched by ten different men would be completely different.

Thatchers have always been very secretive and territorial. Some have been known to get off the roof if anyone was watching. It is said that the only way for an outsider to learn this craft is to marry into it.

Thatch is enjoying a strong revival on the continent of Europe. In England today, there are almost one thousand Master Thatchers and even a few Mistress Thatchers, working full time at their chosen craft.

Hugh O'Neill

Master Thatcher

Connemara, on the west coast, is the one part of Ireland that has remained more pungently itself throughout all the upheavals of the centuries. Here it feels as though history has never found its way down these twisting, narrow roads. Men stand as they have for centuries, huddled over their pints of beer at the local bar. As in all rural Ireland, life revolves around the parish church and the village bar, both of them places where all the family go to meet friends and neighbors. Strangers are treated with a shy friendliness and a genuine interest. Under everchanging skies the offerings of nature stretch one's credulity.

Stone walls divide the green fields into sun-dappled patchwork. Bluebells lie in the woods like small lakes; in rough pastures cowslips are out with their tufts of wrinkled leaves and their yellow flowers at the end of long green bells. Horse chestnut trees are laden with white candles, and the scent of hawthorn flowers mixed with the spicy aroma of bog myrtle wafts down the lanes.

Some roads seem to go on forever, leading to nowhere but the sea.

Donkeys are totally at home in this landscape, as are the golden yellow gorse bushes and the acres of black-brown turf. The undulating mountains in the distance change color with every whim of the sun and sky.

Hugh O'Neill, perhaps the best thatcher in Ireland, lives in this magical part of Ireland. Home is a thatched house built of local stone, overlooking a beautiful bay in Lettermore, County Galway.

When he opens the door of his house in answer to my knock, I notice that Hugh is wearing an Aran sweater, immediately placing him in perfect harmony with his surroundings.

We decide to begin our conversation at the point where about twenty years ago, Hugh, a young man from Waterford, made the decision to travel through Asia.

As yet unsure what his goal in life should be, he felt that traveling to wider

Hugh O'Neill harvesting the water reeds. When dried, they are tied into bundles for thatching.

Hugh O'Neill thatching the roof of the Swiss Cottage.

and different shores might provide the answer. Afghanistan, Turkey, Nepal, India, he visited them all, observing the customs of the indigenous population, their husbandry, their architecture, and their crafts. India was the country in which he spent the most time, and which, in the end, would guide him in the direction his life would take. He was impressed by the manner in which the Indians made use of their natural resources; with very little money at their disposal, they nevertheless fashioned pretty and useful things, both for themselves and to sell.

Admiring the intricacies of Indian architecture and its appropriateness to that country, it occurred to him that we too in Ireland had a native architecture—the thatched house and cottage.

I decided to return to Ireland and to learn the craft of thatching. Within a month of my return, I was apprenticed to Jimmy Moran in Headford, County Galway. He was the last of the traditional thatchers, and I was very lucky that he agreed to teach me. The craft, as it is practiced today, has changed very little since the Middle Ages, so thatched roofs are living examples of vernacular architecture. Thatched dwellings evolved over the centuries from the circular or round house to the rectangular cottages of today.

What remains of the buildings of the monastic period of the seventh and eighth centuries, and the Viking buildings excavated at Wood Quay in Dublin, have left us rich in evidence of construction. But most important of all is the material used.

From the beginning I have always used organically grown materials. I grow my own reed, Phragmites communis, but this year I shall be harvesting a variety of materials, including flax.

I ask, "Is there any one thatching job you have done which has given you more pleasure than any other?" Hugh pauses to think before he replies:

Well, there are several jobs of which I am proud. Certainly one of them is the Swiss Cottage in Cahir, County Tipperary. It is, in fact, a Cottage Ornée, a style brought into fashion by Queen Marie Antoinette, when, yearning for a degree of freedom from the grandeur and tedious formalities of the French court, she conceived the idea of building a village on the grounds of the Petit Trianon, where she and her friends could play out a life of rustic simplicity. All of the buildings had thatched roofs and the outer walls were covered with trellises.

About ten years later the fashion for elaborate rustic cottages crossed the channel to England, and the building of cottages ornées became the new pleasure of the gentry. John Nash was the architect who more than any other adopted this style. In 1810 John Nash was commissioned by the Earl of Glengall to build a cottage ornée on his estate in Cahir.

Over the years it had become vacant and fallen into disrepair. An American lady visiting Ireland saw the cottage and, recognizing its architectural importance, offered to have her family's trust pay for its complete restoration.

I was commissioned to thatch the roof. It was the most elaborate job I have ever undertaken, but the end result was magnificent, even if I say so myself. It is now open to the public, and has a wide appreciative audience.

Curiosity prompted me to ask Hugh: "In my travels around Ireland, I have been very excited by the interest in, and the re-vival of, many of the native crafts. Does this interest extend to thatching?"

Yes indeed. In many instances the thatched cottage has survived, particularly in coastal areas, such as Dunmore East in County Waterford, Kilmore Quay, County Wexford, and the village of Adare in County Limerick. They are good examples of regional vernacular styles.

Thatch is being considered a viable option for new buildings due to its insulating qualities and aesthetic appeal. It can last for more than thirty years, longer than any other roofing material, and it has an added advantage of forming a harmonious feature in the surrounding landscape.

To keep the craft of thatching alive it is necessary to teach younger people the skills. Apprenticeship is still the most effective form of training as it maintains the quality and practices which have been handed down from generation to generation. It is important to teach the apprentices the essence and principles of these traditions, not simply the technique.

I see thatch as a versatile and creative material and a renewable resource which in the future will attract more people to appreciate it for its natural qualities. There is nothing more beautiful than a well-designed building made of natural materials—stone, timber, thatch.

As I left Connemara that evening, I stopped the car to have a last look at its distinctive landscape. The sun was sinking behind the horizon, the bay looked as though it was made of molten gold. It doesn't surprise me that Hugh O'Neill has chosen to live on this periphery of Europe's periphery—here everything seems real after all.

Hugh O'Neill graciously supplied the information for this list of thatching materials and terms.

The term "thatch" refers to any roof made of organic material.

Water reed (*Phragmites communis*) Reeds are mostly found in river estuaries. Most reeds will vary in height from five feet to eight feet. It has a natural tapering quality as it rises from its stem to its seed head. Before mechanical methods of harvesting came into being, it was cut by sickle or hook, and it is still cut this way by some marshmen. Harvesting of reed should not be undertaken until the heavy frost has removed all the leaves; generally it can commence from December and finish when the new shoots appear in the spring. Reed has its own distinctive appearance and quality and can differ from one reed bed to the next. The beds need to be harvested on a yearly or biyearly basis to maintain a good straight quality. When reed is gathered together it is known as a bundle, usually about twenty-four inches in circumference. One such bundle covers approximately one square foot of space on the roof for a twelve-inch thickness of thatch which is the standard thickness. An average Irish cottage would need from six to ten acres of reed bed.

Combed wheat reed This was most commonly used in Ireland as a thatching material prior to the arrival of the threshing mill and later the combine harvester, which has greatly reduced the amount of good length straw for thatching. It has similar qualities to reed, with a neat close-cropped finish, but it has a softer appearance than water reed, and is much more flexible to shape for difficult features. Special long-stemmed varieties are grown for strength and it is cut slightly green by a reaper and binder machine, and then stacked in the field to ripen. It is then put into larger stacks to protect until the grain is removed. The straw is fed through a combing machine that not only removes the grain but also the leaves and any other waste matter. When it comes out of the machine it is tied into sheaves; it is then ready for use. The corn crops, wheat, rye, and oaten straw are used; all will have their own characteristics and color differences. The ideal straw is thirty-six inches or more in length. It is harvested during the summer months. To produce a durable material it needs to be grown organically.

Flax Flax is used in the linen industry in Northern Ireland and thus tends to be used more often in the northern counties.

Ling and sedge Less common materials used.

Hazel and willow Hazel and willow are used to make scallops (pins) to secure thatch to an existing roof and also used to secure the ridge on top of the roof, as it is the most vulnerable area and needs to be firmly netted down.

Thatching Terms

Sheaves Bundles of straw.

Beets Term used for bundles of flax.

Stooks Corn standing in the field after it has been cut and left to dry.

Stacks Corn gathered into larger amounts to be stored until the grain is removed. They were covered with conical tops made from thatch to protect the grain.

Scutching Beating the grain seed out of the straw.

Ridge Roof capping style; will vary according to the region.

Bobbins Straw twisted to create a knob shape which is used to seal the top of ridge.

Bauntaub Eave line when starting the roof.

Blue stone (copper sulphate) Often sprayed over the thatch to kill any algae or insects, and to deter birds.

Spot Board used for cutting reed.

Scollops Twisted hazel and willow twigs used as pins or pegs to hold down thatch.

Stretchers Long lengths of hazel and willow used horizontally across each course of thatch.

Stool Clump of hazel and willow.

Stroke A strip of thatch starting from the eave to the ridge measuring three feet wide.

Scraw Top layer of sod usually put over the rafters to keep a house insulated and to hold down the thatch.

Irish Words

Súgan A straw rope.

Tuiodoir The thatcher.

Tui Thatched cottage.

Meitheal Feast and harvest festival celebrations.

Textiles

Weaving
Knitting
Lacemaking
Irish Linen
Printed Textiles

Weaving

The process of weaving consists of interlacing, at right angles, two or more series of flexible materials, of which the longitudinal are called warp and the transverse weft. Weaving, therefore, only embraces one section of the textile industry, for felted, plaited, netted, hosiery, and lace fabrics lie outside this definition. Woven fabrics are varied in texture and have an enormous range of application. The demands made by prehistoric man for fabrics suitable for clothing and shelter were few and simple, and these were fashioned by interlacing strips of fibrous material and grasses, which in their natural condition were long enough for the purpose in hand. But, as he passed from the age of savagery into a civilized being, his needs developed with his culture, and these needs are still extending. It no longer suffices for individual necessities: luxury, commerce, and many industries must also be considered. The invention of spinning gave a great impetus to the introduction of varied effects. The weaver was called upon to furnish

articles to  suit a whole range of requirements. In colder countries a demand arose for warm

clothing, and in hot ones for cooler material. In order to meet these requests the world continues to search for suitable raw materials. From the animal kingdom, wool, hair, fur, feathers, and silk have long been procured.

*This waisted and belted suit in black and peat brown
handwoven Irish tweed was designed by the author in 1956.*

From the vegetable kingdom, cotton, flax, hemp, jute, and a host of other less known but equally valuable materials are derived. Over the centuries the machines which have been invented to achieve various effects have been numerous, thus offering an almost endless choice for the public to choose from.

As with ceramics the Chinese led the world in the craft of weaving. It is established that as early as 2690 B.C. they were the only cultivators of silk, the delicacy and fineness of which must have postulated possibilities in weaving far beyond those of looms in which grasses, wool, and flax were used. It is therefore probably correct to credit the Chinese with being the earliest inventors of looms for weaving figured silks, which in the course of time other nations (acquainted only with wool and flax textiles) saw with wonder.

Spinning and weaving were introduced to Ireland around five thousand years ago by the Neolithic farmers who crossed the sea in their light curragh-type boats looking for a settled way of life. It is probable that they also introduced sheep to Ireland. Who first thought of using the fleece of the sheep to make clothing is not known, but certainly from earliest times man has kept and bred sheep with this object in view. It is known that in medieval Ireland wool from black sheep was used in the making of garments, because Giraldus Cambrensis, that great chronicler of the twelfth century, remarked of his visit to Ireland that "nearly all the woollen clothing the Irish wore were black, that being the color of the sheep in the country."

These early farmers were the first of a succession of immigrants and invaders who came to these shores and who would shape the history of Ireland and lay the foundation of a way of life, some aspects of which have lasted down to the present day. Toward the end of the Bronze Age, around 500 B.C., the Celts began to arrive.

Like so many other handcrafts the technique of weaving has remained essentially the same for hundreds of years. In 1895 a loom incorporating a fly shuttle was introduced into County Donegal, for woollen weaving, and within a few years this type of loom almost entirely replaced the throw loom.

From the earliest times dyes have been extracted from berries, stems, and leaves, as well as roots and flowers of various plants.

Great skill was required in selecting the plants and in their subsequent use. The women of the household were responsible for dyeing the fleeces, and the knowledge of which plants would give the desired color was handed down from generation to generation. Some of these natural dyes are still used today.

Lichen, the most popular of all the traditional dye stuffs, is a plant organism composed of fungus and alga, and is usually gray-green or yellow in color. It grows on rocks, tree trunks, and walls. For black, the fine, intensely black sediment found at the bottoms of some bogs is used. Blue-black is obtained from blackthorn fruit (sloes), and the root of the yellow iris (saggon), and the bark of certain trees. Brown comes from crottle, a type of lichen found on stones. The shade can be varied by experts from a dark brown, almost black, to a pale fawn. This dye was one of the most popular ones and there was a great demand for material dyed with this substance. While blackberry fruit was used for blue, indigo produced the deepest blues. The wool had to be stewed in the indigo for at least three days to obtain the right intensity of color. Young heather shoots, which gives a pale green color, was only used for flecks and spots of color, as all green cloths had unlucky associations with the fairies. For various shades of yellow, corn marigold or blossoms of the gorse or "whin" were used. Turf soot and alder twigs were used as a mordant which fixed the colors in the wool.

Muriel Gahan

Dr. Muriel Gahan (pronounced Gay-en) was born in 1897. An honorary doctorate from Trinity College, Dublin, was conferred upon her in recognition of outstanding services to Irish handcrafts, weaving in particular. Her long life, which she describes as being of "supreme happiness and contentment," has been dedicated to the recognition and organization of these crafts.

I spent my childhood in Castlebar, County Mayo. My father represented the Congested Districts Board (C.D.B.) in that county, an organization which gave as much assistance as possible to save the weavers from emigration and starvation. We wore homespun garments, partially to encourage the weavers, but also because we loved the colors which were achieved by using natural dyes.

I was educated at Alexandra College in Dublin; it was here that I met a group of girls who became my friends, and later, my co-workers.

In 1926 I came to live in Dublin, to work in a home-decorating business. One of my school-friends, Lucy Franks, had a stand at the Royal Dublin Society's (the R.D.S.) Spring Show and needed a weaver to complement her basketmak-

ers, etc. Hearing that I was about to make a visit to my sister in County Mayo, she asked me if I could find her one. I was looking for a weaver and his loom, who wove tweed made of yarn spun by hand, and who would be willing to travel to Dublin and participate in Lucy's exhibition. We found two in a mountain village behind Newport, but neither of them would travel as far afield as Dublin. Our search ended west of the village of Ballycroy where in a low thatched house we found Peter Madden, the weaver. Yes, he'd come to Dublin. And a loom (for his generation loom was bedded deeply into the floor)? "I'll make you a loom," he said. And he did.

My sister and I had enjoyed our weaver search so much that we decided to look for more people involved in crafts, and to record and evaluate the situation as we found it. After making inquiries we decided to begin our task less than twelve miles from Castlebar, on the way to Achill. We took a mountain road that climbed up high above the waters of a beautiful lake. The silence was such that we could hear the gentle swish of the lake water lapping up against the pebbles of its quiet shore. At the summit we lingered a moment or two in order to admire Clew Bay; from this height its small green islands looked like emeralds glistening in the sun.

Across the bay was Ireland's holy mountain, Croagh Patrick, down which the saint is reputed to have banished the snakes; the pilgrims' way a formidable obstacle course of loose quartz rocks that fell off an iceberg 400 million years ago. Here nature is kept pristine but there is no feeling of loneliness. Our narrow path bore the footprints of human beings going back generations, perhaps even further back, to the earliest of times.

The road now began to descend; there was nothing but heather and rock, but as the valley came more clearly into view, we could see miniature green fields, and an occasional whitewashed cottage. It was here we found our homespun, here, in the heart of the mountains the women were spinning as they had been for hundreds of years past, and men were weaving on the same looms their fathers had used, and their fathers before them.

We met two of the women on the road; when they heard what we were looking for they brought us into their homes, and while they cheered us with strong black tea and currant soda bread, they told us the way of it.

The sheep are shorn in May; those tough little mountain black-faced sheep that swarm over the hills, whose voice on a still day is the only sound in this lonely valley. In Shrahmore, for that is the name of this hidden place, there are also some flocks of Cheviot sheep. Theirs is a ''kind'' wool, the women told us, for it adds a softness to the yarn that the mountain wool lacks.

During the summer the women gather their dyes. The gray lichen off the rocks, the ''moss'' as it is called here, for those wonderful shades ranging from tawny orange to deep red-brown. Heather for yellow, bracken for green, elderberry for purple—there is hardly a flower or berry that does not give some color. All these vegetable dyes give soft beautiful hues, like the rocks and the bogs, and the mountains where they grow. Indigo is the very color of the sky. It was because of indigo that we were here. We had seen a coat of this heavenly blue homespun on a friend, and she had told us that it had come from this valley. We asked our new friends—''Who does the indigo?'' and they directed us across the valley to a tiny cottage half buried in gorse and rushes. Nearby, a narrow stream tumbled with amazing ferocity down the mountainside, and we found her there, washing her wool. Some of it was spread out to dry on the whins, like a great ragged sheep caught in the bushes. We knew she was a fairy when we saw her. Unlike the other women she was wearing a scarlet tweed petticoat, a black shawl was draped over her shoulders and a white cloth tied around her head. Her face was seamed with a thousand wrinkles, and smiles ran out of her eyes and around her mouth. She was less than four feet tall. She guided us back to her cottage, and barefooted, she danced rather than walked along beside us. She told us about her flock of lovely white Cheviots, and the soft wool she got from them to spin her yarn. The indigo was hard to come by now, she said, but not long since she had come across a lump of it in the roof.

Looking up at the roof, shining black as ebony through the mysterious wreathing blue of the turf smoke, we would have felt no surprise at anything coming out of it. A girl was carding wool in the chimney corner. ''A neighbor,'' the fairy told us. On the fire a black three-legged pot was boiling. It was wool being dyed with the moss. The house was filled with the smell of it. This dye needs no mordant, unlike most vegetable dyes that need to be mixed with alum, or some chemical, in order to fix the color. ''The neighbor'' showed us the carders. They were like two square flat-backed brushes with short wire bristles. After dyeing the wool is dried, then

A coat of whitewashed handwoven Irish tweed designed in 1951.

teased and carded. Carding is hard, tedious work she told us. The wool is drawn between the carder and made into soft rolls ready for spinning.

It is the big spinning wheels they use here. The spinner walks backward and forward, twirling the wool between her fingers. In Donegal they use the small flax wheels. That work is done sitting at the wheel, and the wool can be spun more finely than on the other types.

The fairy took down from the beam in the ceiling a huge ball of yarn she had just spun. It was beautifully fine and strong, in spite of the big wheel. The next day the yarn was being sent off to the weaver four miles over the mountain. One weaver can do the work for ten to fifteen spinners, she told us. If he is a good worker he will do over twenty yards in two days, whereas it will have taken her three weeks to prepare that amount of yarn. After it has been woven, the tweed goes back again to the spinner, and she washes it and shrinks it, and rolls it ready for sale. The shrinking is done by leaving the tweed out on a wall and letting the sun and rain do their work.

Listening to all these kind mountain people

we began to understand the important part the woman takes in making a piece of homespun. Nine-tenths of the work is hers. There is, of course, good weaving and bad weaving, but it is the dyeing and spinning that make the real difference between a good and bad homespun.

We said good-bye to our fairy at last, and we carried away with us the echoing sound of her voice, as she sped barefoot up the mountain calling to her white sheep.

Farther west, but still in County Mayo, on a day of driving rain and mist, we came to a house in a bog. The roof was of sods, and so low were the walls, and so covered with moss, that we would have passed it by, but for the red light that shone out through the open door. A weaver lived there all alone. He told us the light was burning to St. Anthony, the poor man's friend. An ancient loom stretched from wall to wall, but the only light he had to work by was the red light of his saint and the glow of the turf fire. He wove floor rugs of great beauty and original design out of homespun wool which he dyed himself. He had the fire of a zealot burning in his eyes, and he had a vision of all Ireland being carpeted in his rugs.

In the Aran Islands thirty miles west of Galway, we found the oldest weaving in Europe: multicolored belts worn by men and women, woven between the fingers without any loom. But the yarn was not homespun, it was bought in a shop in Galway. The colors were crude and ugly. We carried away one unforgettable picture of Aran. It was our last day, and we were hurrying to Kilronan to catch the boat to the mainland. Suddenly over the brow of the hill, silhouetted against a vivid blue sky, a man on horseback appeared riding toward us, a big bronzed beautiful man dressed in white from head to toe—white wool tam-o'-shanter and jersey, jacket and trousers of white homespun, on

his feet were white goat-hair pampooties [shoes], and he rode into the sunlight on a white horse.

We found some homespun in all the western counties, Galway, Kerry, Clare, and Sligo, but very little of it. Most of the Galway and Kerry tweed, wrongly called homespun, is handwoven of mill-spun yarn. It lacks the interest and beauty of hand-spun tweed, that rough-surfaced uneven look showing the hand of the craftsman, the look that spinning mills the world over try to imitate.

Our search ended in Donegal. We arrived there in the early autumn over miles of purple brown bog, with the mountain Errigal rising like a spear in the distance. It was when we got to the blue lake at the foot of Errigal that we knew we had reached the land of the spinners: a splash of scarlet on a gray wall, the steady whirr of a wheel coming from an open door— Dunlewy, the heart of the Donegal homespun country. Here every woman spins, and there is work in this district for three, perhaps four, weavers.

In the last few years, great strides have been made in the homespun industry in Donegal. Girls and young men have been apprenticed to older spinners and weavers. Spinning competitions have been held, and the women have been encouraged to keep record books of their dye plants and colors. They experiment with every kind of flower; one woman showed us many beautiful shades of red, ranging from the softest pink that she had got using different mordants to the fuchsia that grows in the hedges all along the roadside.

The tweed here is harsher than the Mayo tweed. It is purely mountain wool, but its hardness is also a virtue, for it stands up to the weather and the rain can hardly penetrate its tough surface. It is always in mountain districts that homespun is found. The mountain people, cut off from the rest of the world, have had to spin and weave to clothe themselves and their children, and so the homespun has survived. It is here too that the Irish language is still alive; it is the speech of their everyday life.

These people are the kindest in the world, and one of the most industrious, but they are living a hundred years too late. They are at the mercy of a world governed by advertising slogans and quick sale returns. Unable to go in search of a market, they are dependent on the trade that stops at their doors: a letter with a chance order, a passing tourist, and many of them live in such remote places that a tourist would not venture there.

"How are these people to make a living?" "How is this age-old industry to be saved for the country?" These were the questions I was asking myself—the answers were nearer than I realized.

A couple of weeks later some friends joined me in a lodge we shared near Headford on Lough Corrib. The homespun webs were admired by everyone, and we got talking of the plight of the isolated craftworker cut off from any market. That was when the idea was born of starting a sales depot in Dublin for homespuns and other crafts.

Lucy Franks, who had been delighted with the weaver we had got for her stand at the Spring Show, was equally delighted with our plans for a craft sales depot which was also to sell work done by the United Irishwomen. This name was shortly afterward changed to The Irish Countrywomen's Association Ltd. "Why not," she wrote, "sell lunches and teas as well."

My job was to find a place in Dublin for our depot and get it going. A dust-covered "to let" notice in the basement of a Georgian house on St. Stephen's Green brought me and the estate agent stumbling down gloomy steps. The whole place was so neglected and desolate as to fill one with the elation which the prospect of any desperate venture evokes. Without any doubt this was the place for us.

Our entire capital was £500, which had to cover decoration, equipment, and furniture and all else needed to start a business. The cheapest contractor we could find pulled down and put up partitions. For the next seven months we were lost to our families, never reaching home until midnight. We were ready for our opening on December 1, 1930. Shortly thereafter, we registered as a private company, Country Workers Limited, "a company formed for the development of Irish country crafts and kindred projects, and from which no profit is taken for private gain." From the first, any profit made in the restaurant was used to help our country work by means of grants, instruction, prizes and the like. Profit on craft sales went back to the workers as an annual Christmas bonus.

In the spring of 1935 we went to London to see an exhibition of English country crafts. "Could we not have the same in Dublin," we asked ourselves—well, why not?

Country Workers Ltd., from its own resources, could not finance an exhibition of the ambitious size contemplated, and our thoughts turned to the Royal Dublin Society. Our request for help brought the Society's Honorary Secretary in person—Professor Felix Hackett whose zeal in the cause of craftsmanship had been a strength to our work from the start. Dr. Hackett's message was that the R.D.S. could not give us, a private company, help with the exhibition, but if we were to form a voluntary society of like-minded people something might be done the following year.

The new society was formed and named by June. Its name, The Irish Homespun Society,

*A selection of colorful handwoven Irish tweeds
made by Magee and Company of Donegal.*

and its equivalent in Irish—An Cumann Sniomachain—was given it because its primary purpose was the development of the homespun industry in the Gaeltacht (Irish speaking area).

In October 1935 the society organized a small exhibition of homespuns and other crafts in the Country Shop, financed by Country Workers. It had far-reaching results. Mr. Connolly, Minister for Lands, and Mr. Moran, Director of the Gaeltacht Services, came to see it and invited the society to send a memorandum to the government on the homespun industry. Mr. Ingram, head of Technical Instruction, also came to see it, and offered his help in every possible way—help in which his branch of the Department of Education has never failed from that day.

Mr. Bohane, Director of the Royal Dublin So-

Weaving

ciety, came to see the exhibition, and told us that we could count on a favorable reply to our request for help to hold an exhibition at the Spring Show the following year. In the years following, it is to the Royal Dublin Society above all others that the Homespun Society owes the opportunities of doing the work for which it was founded.

In 1946 the Homespun Society was invited to stage an exhibition at the Horse Show instead of the Spring Show, and in Pembroke Hall instead of the Members Hall. This exhibition was visited by Dr. Seamus Delargy, Director of the Folklore Commission. Wearing a look of amazement he stood in the hall looking around him at traditional crafts of every kind, at spinners and weavers working at their looms and wheels, at basketmakers, the blacksmith, the chairmaker, the stone-carver, all part of the material folk culture, almost as dear to him as the folklore to which he had given his life—and saying as he looked, "Everyone should know about this."

The Homespun Society organized many more exhibitions later, in different places, but no more at the Royal Dublin Society, whose invitation for the following year was regretfully refused. After the 1946 exhibition it was felt by us all that the time had come to organize production in the country rather than hold exhibitions in the city. The Homespun Society now remains in the background as an educational committee concerned with craftsmanship. It has handed on its other work to Country Markets, which in 1945 it formed jointly with the Irish Countrywomen's Association.

Spring 1952 brought an invitation to lunch from Dr. Hayes, a fellow member of the Arts Council. During lunch he told me that there were two representatives of the Kellogg Foundation on their way to Dublin. "They want to help something in Ireland," he said, "and I thought you might have something in mind for the country."

"Something in mind." My thoughts ranged over the fields covered by the Arts Council. The visual arts, perhaps help with a craft designer, or an organizer? Maybe something like the English Rural Industries Bureau? No, that was too ambitious. Traveling organizers in music and drama? There was no indication of what the Kellogg Foundation's interests were. What about agriculture? Country Markets badly needed a market organizer. Then there were the Home Economics Advisers we had asked for in the Irish Countrywomen's Association, and greatest of all our needs—a permanent residential college—too ambitious by far.

The day of the lunch party came and my mind was still roaming. Dr. Morris, President of the W. K. Kellogg Foundation, and his colleague couldn't have been more friendly, and conversation was easy and general. Then suddenly all other thoughts left me except those of our Country Women's College. They listened to the account of our summer school and college moving from place to place, and of the plan we had put to the government for a permanent college, and our ideas of what we wanted. And it appeared that Denman, the Woman's Institute's Country Women's College in England was known to them, and that the foundation itself had a college of adult education in Michigan. The whole conception of our college was tangible and understood by them. Dr. Morris asked for more details to be sent to him.

In June we sent the foundation the original memorandum of a permanent residential college which we had submitted to the Departments of Agriculture and External Affairs some months before. The dream became a reality. The Irish Countrywomen's Association got its residential college, An Grianan (translated it means "The

Sunny Place''), a gift from the W. K. Kellogg Foundation, unconditional except that we should use it right away. This wonderful gift was our first experience of the Kellogg Foundation's boundless goodwill and generosity which it has been our privilege to enjoy from that time.

An Grianan had been going for several months when I asked Dr. Hayes why his choice had fallen on me when he was considering causes that needed help. ''Well,'' he said, ''it was really Dr. Delargy of the Folklore Commission. He was always talking about the work you were doing in the country with the crafts and exhibitions and everything—and then, do you remember the meeting we had?'' Yes, I remember the meeting. It was before we knew that the Arts Council was being set up, and we talked about a special kind of Folk Museum where there would be rooms for music, poetry, and dancing, as well as the more usual occupations and crafts.

My mind went back to that Royal Dublin Society exhibition and Dr. Delargy looking around happily at the traditional craftsmen and craftswomen at work, and his remark, ''Everyone should know about this.''

And that is why a resolution went into An Grianan records ''that the encouragement and development of our Irish traditional crafts should always be part of An Grianan's work, and it is another reason why Irish art, music, literature, and language must always have a place in our college.''

Helena Ruuth

Weaver

Helena Ruuth's delicate beauty is reflected in the exquisite stoles, scarves, and throws she designs in her studio, which occupies most of the garden level of the large Victorian house she shares with her husband, the writer Wesley Burrows, one son, one daughter, and a bevy of much-loved family dogs.

Visiting the studio one is dazzled by a feast of color and texture: baskets overflow with brightly colored balls of yarn—woollens, alpacas, mohairs, linens, silks, and even some mink. Experimenting with designs, which she will eventually send out to a weaver, she leaves notes for herself pinned to the side of the loom, as though fearful she might forget a fleeting moment of inspiration. I am curious to know how it was that Helena, a graduate in Textile Design from the Stockholm College of Art, came to live and work in Ireland. In answer to my question she explains:

In the early sixties a group of Scandinavian designers were asked to report on the state of design in Ireland, and their report—a highly critical one—was the basis of the setting up of the Kilkenny Design Workshops. The head of Textiles at the Swedish College of Art was asked to recommend someone who might establish the weaving section of the workshops, whose function was to instigate a greater awareness of design in Irish manufacture. I was recommended for this post and arrived in Kilkenny in the summer of 1965.

My brief was to produce prototypes for new products which would then be offered to Irish textile manufacturers, who would thus be encouraged to introduce new design elements which would enable them to increase their sales potential, particularly in the export markets.

I worked with four different companies including the Irish Tapestry Company of Drogheda. For the latter I designed a bedspread, now known as the Kilkenny Bedspread, a high-quality

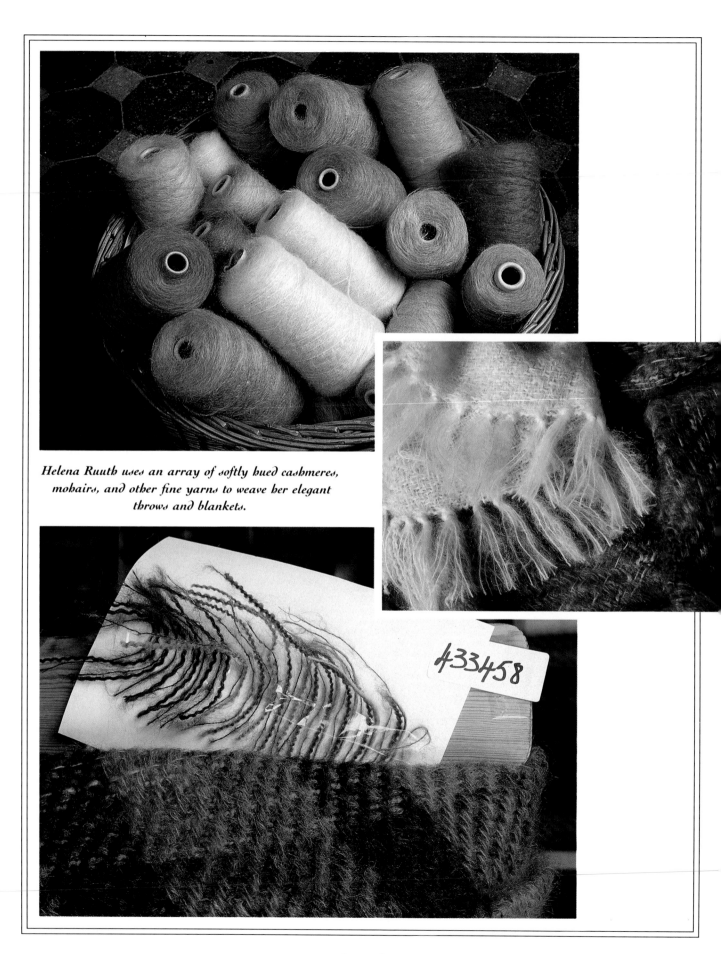

Helena Ruuth uses an array of softly hued cashmeres, mohairs, and other fine yarns to weave her elegant throws and blankets.

all-wool product which is still in production and used by architects for many projects in Ireland, and overseas.

After two years in Kilkenny I set up my own design studio with my own production. At the same time I continued to design in a free-lance capacity. I was invited by Terence Conran, proprietor of Habitat in England, to design a range of upholstery fabrics for the public and private furnishings in Heathrow Airport.

My own company, Helena Ruuth Limited, specializes in handwoven, and also hand-knitted, products. The work of this company has achieved a high reputation in the field of exclusive weaves and knits. In 1987, for instance, I won the Crafts Council Award (Best Software) at the National Craft Trade Fair in the Royal Dublin Society from more than six hundred exhibitors.

Helena's outlets are in the most prestigious stores, not only in Ireland but abroad, particularly in the United States and Japan—Bloomingdale's, Neiman Marcus, Macy's, all carry her designs, as do Isetan of Tokyo, Yagi Tsusho of Osaka, and Wakabyashi of Tokyo.

She has designed and made large woven wall hangings for hotel interiors.

Other commissions have included woven wall hangings for the Irish Embassy in Washington, D.C., and for several boardrooms in Ireland and abroad, and carpets for Seanad Eireann, at Leinster House, the seat of the Irish parliament. There have been textiles for many hotels and an especially interesting project was the coordination of interior textiles for the new A320 Airbus fleet of Guinness Peat Aviation and other aircraft for the same company.

"What do you consider to have been your most challenging commission?" I ask Helena. She replies: "Perhaps my most challenging commission was that of designing the large tapestry backdrop for the Pope's Mass in Drogheda in September 1979. The original tapestry now hangs in St. Peter's Church, Drogheda."

Probably Helena Ruuth is the most successful designer-weaver in Ireland today. She wears her success lightly; one cannot help but feel that true contentment for Helena lies in the quiet moments when she is creating glorious items for the world to enjoy.

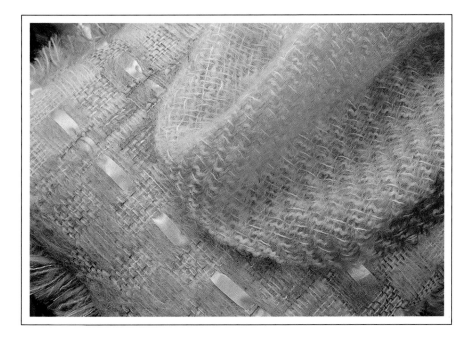

Knitting

The origins of knitting have been lost in the mists of time, but historians have concluded that it was invented by the Arabs more than two thousand years ago. While it was the  Arab traders who brought knitting to Europe, it was the monks who spread the craft across the Continent and to Ireland together with the gospel of Christianity. One theory suggests that the garment worn by Jesus Christ at the time of his crucifixion was a knitted one, the argument being, that according to the scriptures it was a "seamless garment," which could only mean that it was knitted in the round and hence they had to "cast lots for it" because it could not be divided. Until the sixteenth century only men were knitters throughout Europe. Women spun the flax and various animal fibers into woollen yarns. The craft reached its peak during the Middle Ages and early Renaissance period, and became one of the basic industries across Europe. To become a master knitter a young man had to serve an arduous apprenticeship that lasted for six years. During the first three years he was taught the rudiments of the craft, during the second three he traveled extensively all over Europe, studying the works of many master knitters. When his six years were  completed the apprentice was ready for acceptance to the

Guild of Knitters, but he had yet to undergo a demanding test—in a limited period of thirteen weeks he had to knit the following items: a carpet in a colored design containing flowers, foliage, birds, and animals (the carpet had to measure six feet by five feet, approximately), a felted woollen beret, a woollen shirt, and a pair of hose that would fit his size. The completed test pieces were then submitted to the Council of the Guild, and if they received the approval of the Council, the title of Master Knitter was bestowed on him. This allowed him to set up a business of his own and to hang the sign of the Master Knitter outside his workshop. The sign consisted of a stocking on which were drawn vertical lines, and across the top of the stocking were a few horizontal lines—these were the origin of the stockinette stitch and the garter stitch. It is from these two that all other knitting stitches are derived.

The first mention of a woman knitting was in the year 1589—she was a Mrs. Lee, wife of Rector William Lee. The rector saw his wife knitting with her needles from early morning until rushlight, and this inspired him to invent "a machine" which would take the drudgery out of hand-knitting. Within a few short years this machine breathed new life into knitting all over Europe, and in a slightly altered form is in use today in factories across the world.

Different countries specialized in different types of knitting. In England the knitting of hosiery was one of the main industries. In France and Belgium lace knitting flourished, in Germany and Austria heavy cable and bobble stitches were produced. In Holland embossed knitted fabrics created very interesting effects—animals, birds, and flowers were worked in reverse stockinette stitch on a stockinette-stitch foundation. In Scandinavia the hand-knitters copied, in knitting, the reindeer and trees which were part of their natural background. The multicolored knitting which the Arab traders brought to Spain traveled from Spain to Fair Isle in Scotland, and this Spanish tradition still lingers there to the present day. In fact, all genuine Fair Isle knits should have the Armada Cross as one of its basic motifs.

In the early part of the nineteenth century a Mrs. Jessie Scanlon visited the Shetland Islands and brought with her a collection of laces which she had gathered from all parts of Europe. Even though the laces were made with lace needles, the Shetlanders who were ardent hand-knitters, were soon busy copying the patterns from Mrs. Scanlon's laces and were reproducing them with their knitting needles.

Traditional Irish knitting, also known as Aran knitting, is easily recognizable by its off-white color and embossed patterns. There are two reasons why it is called Aran knitting. The first and well-known one is the fact that this type of knitting was done on the Aran Islands, off the west coast of Ireland. Less known is that during the latter part of the nineteenth century, after the Great Famine, Congested Districts Boards were set up in various parts of Ireland in an effort to give part-time employment to the underprivileged. One such board was set up in Ballina, County Mayo, and it was managed by Lady Arran who resided there at the time. She organized women to make hand-knitted sweaters using the various embossed patterns which were commonly used in the area, and these people always

Diamonds signify wealth, and the fisherman and his wife always hoped for a wealth of fish.

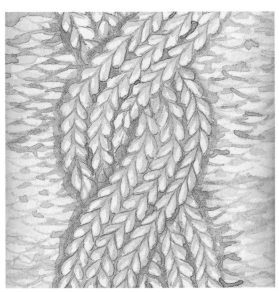

Cables represent the fisherman's ropes, and this stitch comes in many shapes and sizes.

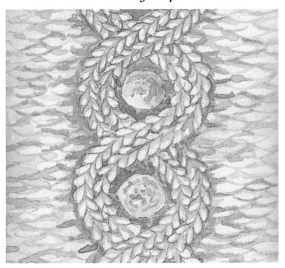

Double zigzag represents the ups and downs of married life, which in all cases would be accepted philosophically.

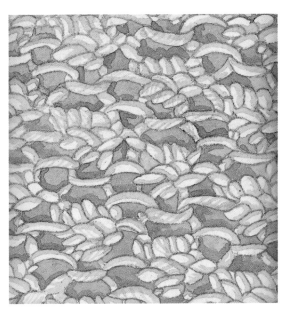

The Trinity stitch (also called the blackberry stitch or popcorn stitch) represents the invocation of the Blessed Trinity and was for the protection of fishermen. The Blessed Trinity means Three Divine Persons in One God, and the actual Trinity stitch is made by knitting three times into the one stitch. It is the most intricate of all the stitches and cannot be reproduced by a machine.

referred to their knitting as Arran knitting because it was Lady Arran who examined the garments, collected them, and paid the hand-knitters. At that time the traditional knitting was done all along the west coast of Ireland stretching from North Donegal right down to South Kerry. In fact, after the famine there were thousands of destitute families and it was the hand-knitting, together with other handcrafts, worked on by the women of Ireland, which reduced many of the hardships attached to poverty.

The Aran sweater, or Aran gansey, as it is referred to in Gaelic-speaking areas, is essentially a protective garment. It is made from natural creamy colored yarn which is known as Bainin (pronounced Baw-neen), which means off-white. The oil put into the fleece at the time of carding is not taken out when this yarn is knitted; as a result it makes for a weatherproof garment suitable for fishermen. It is interesting to note that it was part of a bride's dowry that she be able to knit, and she proved this by knitting a Bridal Sweater for the bridegroom. Each family had its own arrangement of patterns, and the Bridal Sweater always incorporated one of the stitches from the bride's family and some of those from the groom's family, thus setting up a new pattern arrangement for the new family. It is said that if a fisherman were lost at sea, the body could always be identified by the stitches on his Aran sweater.

The stitches which dictate the pattern have a significance beyond mere ornamentation, for they echo the religious beliefs which the majority of the islanders practice. The various stitches also have particular meanings for the fishermen and their wives.

Tarlach de Blacam
Inis Meáin Knitwear

The Aran Islands, Inis Oírr, Inis Meáin, and Inis Mór, are situated beyond the wide sweep of Galway Bay, where sea meets sky in a great arc that embraces everywhere the ancients trod.

Seamus Heaney, the Irish poet, has described them as stepping-stones out of Europe, and that is how they must appear on a map, three islands surrounded by the clear green waters of the Atlantic Ocean lying beyond the periphery of Europe's periphery. J. M. Synge was intoxicated by the life and language of the people of Aran. These haunting islands inspired him to write two of his most successful and enduring plays, *Riders to the Sea* and *The Playboy of the Western World.*

Tourism now earns the islands more than agriculture and fishing, but farming, even on such inhospitable soil, is still the heart of the islands, a tradition begun by the Stone Age settlers who tended their stock, built their monuments, and made necklaces of sheep's teeth, a

thousand years before the Egyptians thought of the pyramids.

It is believed that the west of Ireland has more stone walls per acre than any comparable area in the world. On the Aran Islands there is one material only and that is stone, from which the inhabitants have created one of the most distinctive examples of unspoiled landscape in Western Europe. The stone walls suggest a long and patient seduction of the land to agriculture. One wonders what sort of man had the tenacity to build such walls, like a giant jigsaw, each stone seems to have been chosen with infinite care; there is no cement, just stone upon stone. How can the walls survive the ferocious storms which sweep across the Atlantic, during the winter? Somehow they do, a compliment to the craftsmen who assembled them; they are monuments to human endeavor.

In the early 1950s, a cream-colored woollen

sweater, or gansy, as it is called by the islanders, the traditional garb of their fishermen for at least a hundred years, made the name Aran world-famous. Almost half a century later, knitwear from the Aran Islands is once again receiving attention from the international fashion press, but this time around, the focus is on Inis Meáin, the middle and perhaps least known of the three islands.

The story of Inis Meáin Knitwear started more than twenty years ago, in Dublin, where Tarlach de Blacom, a Trinity College graduate in Celtic languages, met Aine Ní Chongaile (translated it reads Coneely), a teacher at Scoil Lorcáin. They were both involved in the Gaeltacht Civil Rights movement. They married, and when Aine was expecting their first child Ruadhri, they decided to make their home on Inis Meáin, because neither wanted to bring up a child in a city. Aine is a native of Inis Meáin and her family still lives there.

Detail of intricate Aran knitting.

Twenty years ago life on Inis Meáin had changed little over the centuries. The island had no running water and no electricity. The sole means of communication with the mainland was a primitive telephone system and a ferry service that, because it depended on the weather, was erratic, to say the least. Deliveries of cargo were rowed to and from the island in curraghs, the traditional canoe-shaped boat.

Originally Tarlach was employed by the Irish government to manage the community cooperative. There were many challenges to be met, but he threw himself wholeheartedly into bringing Inis Meáin into the twentieth century. In a few years he managed to raise sufficient money to bring electricity and running water to the island, to improve the fledgling air service between the mainland and Inis Meáin and to enlarge the entrance to the harbor, enabling bigger boats to bring in cargo. Despite these achievements, Tarlach realized that something had to be done to stem the tide of emigration of the young people to the mainland.

Tarlach recalls how he and Aine would sit for hours on the beautiful clean beaches, admiring the coastline formed by the elemental forces of the Atlantic, at the same time looking long and hard at the sea as a possible source of income. Most of the islanders made a living from a mixture of farming and fishing. The Atlantic yielded a plentiful supply of fish: mackerel to fresh lobster and wild salmon. But, for many, the fisherman's hard life was not the answer.

Among the island women there was a strong tradition of knitting. In 1977 with no background in design, and in a stone shed lent by a farmer, eight local knitters set to work making the traditional Aran sweaters for tourists who visited the island, but tourism is mercurial; it varies from season to season. Eight years later, Tarlach realized that if knitting was to become a major source of income for the island, the sweaters would have to be exported. It is characteristic of the man that having made his mind up on a particular issue, he will pursue it with the thoroughness of a natural trailblazer.

The knitting enterprise had started as an extension of the coop project; in 1985 Tarlach took over the factory, installed the latest knitting machinery, the first of its kind in the country, and proceeded to make lightweight jacquard sweaters in luxury yarns. The only way to test their saleability was to show them at Italy's premier knitwear show in Florence, a venue visited by the world's most sophisticated knitwear buyers. Pondering over how he would display his work, he happened to notice a curragh drying on the beach, an everyday sight on the islands; but now it gave him the idea of bringing one of these traditional boats to Florence to display the sweaters.

It was a sensation; there was nothing like it in the whole exhibition. The buyers gathered around Tarlach's stand like bees swarming around a hive. Here was this wonderful knitwear made from luxury yarns imported from China, South America, and northern Ireland, in colors which echoed their native landscape, and all displayed on this incredible boat.

Buyers could hardly wait to place their orders; journalists, scenting a good story, hovered around furiously taking notes; European and Japanese television crews were trying to make firm dates to visit Inis

Meáin; all were intrigued, and anxious to make "the journey to the island on the edge of the world." In due time buyers, journalists, photographers, and film crews all came to Inis Meáin and were totally captivated by the island, by the knitwear, and last, but not least, by Tarlach and Aine.

Choosing to live on a remote island, Tarlach has for the past ten years worked with a consultant, Geraldine Clark from Northumberland. She attends the important yarn and knitwear shows and keeps Tarlach informed of the color and shape of the trends in fashion. But the final collection is what Tarlach feels is right.

Everything has to be imported. Once, sometimes twice, a day Tarlach drives his Land Rover down to the harbor, or the airstrip, to collect a new shipment of yarns, linen from northern Ireland (one of the most beautiful sweaters in a recent collection is made with a mixture of pure silk and pure linen), fine worsteds from Yorkshire, or alpaca from Peru. The Inis Meáin logo is appropriately three men carrying a curragh across a strand. Machinery, the most up-to-date Tarlach could find, has been imported to help supply orders, but all of the knitwear is hand-finished. Quality is of the utmost importance.

Initially the sweaters were made for men, the buyers read like a litany of the best men's shops across the world, Neiman Marcus, Paul Smith, and Frank Stella in the United States, Harrods in London, Seibu in Japan and San Francisco, and Smalto in Paris. Tarlach has introduced a collection of knitwear for women and it was an instant success.

Every January and February Tarlach travels to trade fairs. He now produces thirty thousand sweaters a year, 95 percent of which are exported to countries such as Germany, France, Italy, Britain, Japan, and the United States. This year his sales hit the magical million pound mark.

Apart from the months that Tarlach has to travel attending trade fairs, the second drawback to living on an island is, that like most island families, they have to send their children to the mainland for a secondary school education. Both boys, Ruadhri and Eoin, hope to spend their lives on Inis Meáin.

Of the future Tarlach says: "The next decade will be fabulous for knitters because knitwear is going to be very, very big. Sweaters will be worn instead of jackets. It all has to do with casual dressing."

For a recent collection he has returned to the original Aran sweater, taking details from the traditional stitches—moss, blackberry, cable, and tree-of-life. Worked in the subtle colors of the island and knitted from the purest luxury yarns, these sweaters have charm and an element of romance that makes them irresistible.

Early guild sign of a master knitter.

Cyril Cullen
Knitter

My first meeting with Cyril Cullen was in Lismore, a small town in County Waterford, sometime in the early 1970s.

Fred Astaire, the dancer, had a sister, Adele; she had been his first and only dancing partner until she left the stage to marry Lord Charles Cavendish and came to live in Lismore Castle on the banks of the Blackwater River. Visiting her there one weekend, I found Adele very excited about the work of a young knitter living in the town; he had been invited to tea so I could see his work. The knitter was Cyril Cullen, and I was suitably impressed with what I saw. During tea he told me a little about himself.

He was not, in fact, a knitter by trade; he was in Lismore as a higher executive officer of the civil service. However, from the time he was a young boy, while watching his mother and sisters at their knitting, he felt a strong attraction to the craft—an attraction he kept secret because he knew of no other boy, or man, with a sim-

ilar interest. As he grew older his fascination with knitting increased. "I found that my head was bursting with new ideas for knitting stitches and designs that simply would not go away." He began to study the history of the craft, and in the process learned that in Europe, up to the sixteenth century, knitting was practiced exclusively by men; he wasn't a freak after all, simply a throwback to earlier times. His interest aroused, he continued to pursue the history of knitting, a quest that led him to visit many European countries before returning to Ireland.

The tea party at Lismore Castle was to be a turning point in Cyril's life.

It followed that all of Adele's fifty guests were introduced to his knitwear, and as a result he found himself desperately searching for knitters who could help him fill the orders which ensued. Another of Cyril's interests was music. He had trained as a classical pianist and was director of the local ladies' choir. He took the opportunity to suggest that some of them might like to volunteer for his knitting classes. Five of the ladies agreed to do so. The demand for his work continued to grow, to the point where he realized that he had reached a crossroad; he made the decision to abandon the civil service in order to devote all his time to knitwear designing and production.

Looking around for a base for his craft, Cyril found a dilapidated eighteenth-century house in Carrick-on-Shannon, County Leitrim, which he was able to purchase for a reasonable sum. He set about restoring the house to its former glory, converting the outhouses at the back into a studio and workshop. Today, the twenty-one room mansion is fully restored and it is where Cyril lives with his beautiful wife, Margie, and their four daughters, Emily, Benita, Tara, and Margot.

Word reached me that Cyril had acquired a flock of rare Jacob sheep, with the intention of using the yarn spun from their fleece for his knitwear. To provide grazing, he had also acquired a small hillside farm at Cornashamsogue (translated it means "hill of the shy Mayflower"), so-called because each year in the month of May, the base of the hedgerows are carpeted with this small white flower.

Curious to see the Jacob sheep, I decide it is time to accept Cyril's invitation, issued at intervals over the years, to visit him in Carrick-on-Shannon.

On a cold but sunny morning in November, David Davison, the photographer, and I set out for County Leitrim, a distance of about a hundred miles northwest of Dublin. As with most counties in Ireland, Leitrim abounds with myths and

Gerry Dolan and his flock of Jacob sheep.

legends. One such legend has it that Ireland's original craftspeople, the Tuatha de Danaan, came from Leitrim. It is said that they came down in a cloud of mist from the slopes of Sliabh an Iarann (the Iron Mountain which borders Lough Allen), amazing the natives with the skill of their handcrafts, a skill which earned them the name of the "magical people."

Leitrim and its neighboring counties of Cavan, Monaghan, and Sligo are sometimes referred to as the Lake District of Ireland; certainly they share an abundance of beautiful lakes and waterways. Each year whooper swans from Iceland and Bewick's swans from Siberia make their epic migratory flight to winter in the sanctuary of these lakes. W. B. Yeats and other poets have written about the swans; how they glide, aloof and elegant, along the lakes and rivers, their trailing feathers causing a mild ripple over the still waters.

The narrow drumlin hills, Sheebeg and Sheemore (translated from the Gaelic they mean little hill and big hill), are purported to belong to the fairies. Turlough O'Caro-

lan, the famous seventeenth- and eighteenth-century composer of music, named his first composition "Sheebeg Sheemore." He lies buried just a few miles from the hills which were his inspiration.

At this early hour, the road to Carrick-on-Shannon is virtually free of traffic. Overhead the sky has about it the utterly blank pristine blueness of a winter's day. Night frost and morning sun bring out the last color in the leaves; in fieldside hedges pale yellow maple leaves aglow with a luminous intensity, and mingle with the deep purple of the dogwood.

Having faithfully followed Cyril's directions, we are signaling our arrival by knocking at the Cullens' hall door shortly after nine A.M. In November the hours of daylight are few, so pausing, at Margie's behest, only to partake of a cup of piping-hot coffee and mince pie, and to exchange our shoes for woollen stockings and Wellingtons, we quickly get under way to the farm.

The shepherd had not expected us quite so early, so having sent word of our arrival, we begin to climb in the direction where we hope the sheep will be—the Cullens'

Irish Hands

four daughters leaping up the hill like long-legged gazelles, Cyril, David, and I following at a more sedate pace. We walked and walked, straight up sheer hills, over turfy lichen-covered terrain until we came to the small house that Cyril had built, where, when the children were younger, they had picnicked and spent nights.

We sat on rocks and tree stumps while Cyril and two of his daughters went farther up the hill to look for the sheep.

From this vantage point there is a superb view of Lough Allen, one of the largest and most beautiful lakes in Ireland. It is a day of Arcadian light and clarity, the dazzling winter sun, low in the sky, imparting magic to everything it touches. Such a glimpse of nature often briefly caught can stay with one forever. No one spoke, partly because we were a little breathless from the climb, but also, I think there was an awareness of a sort of spiritual sustenance that comes from experiencing solitude in a magnificent landscape.

The faint sound of a dog barking, followed a moment later by the muffled tones of running hooves, announces the welcome arrival of the farmer and his dog. With admirable efficiency their combined skills rounded up the sheep in a matter of minutes, and David was able to get his photographs.

On the way back to Cyril's house, he discusses with me the distinctions of the Jacob sheep.

They are an ancient and unique breed with two or four and sometimes six horns. Their fleece is a patchwork of many natural colors. Mentioned in the Book of Genesis—Joseph's many-colored coat was made from the fleece of the Jacob sheep. When shorn the fleeces are divided into three different sections, one for the off-white colors, one for mid-gray colors, and one for the dark colors. They are then spun into three separate colored yarns using the "woollen spun" method where the fibers remain in their natural state, as opposed to the "worsted spun" method where the fibers are treated. Yarns are then lightly scoured so that some of the original oils are retained. They are now ready for knitting.

I get my inspiration for my collection of Jacob

Cyril Cullen with his four daughters wearing sweaters made from Jacob's sheep wool. Margie Cullen in one of Cyril's colorful sweaters.

jerseys [sweaters] from watching color combinations on the back of the sheep, and in many of the Jacob designs I have put uneven patches of natural colors in the jumpers. To do this effectively the "stitches" are knitted in a transverse manner, resulting in the sleeves and the body of the jumper being all in one piece. The cuffs and basques are knitted separately and then joined with a chain stitch. In this way the knitters can produce the multicolored garment from the one sheep without using any dye.

Returning to Cyril's house via the back entrance, we proceed to the workshops, the place where Cyril's talent and the wool from the sheep unite to make a whole.

The interior looks more like a museum to knitting than a workplace. Fleece waiting to be spun on spinning wheels—some of them more than a hundred years old—carders which prepare the wool for spinning, shuttles, and even a half-finished sock being knitted on eighteenth-century needles—what a wonderful place in which to work; no wonder the knitters are all smiling.

As we walk back to the main house, Cyril tells me that he exports to many countries around the world, usually taking Margie with him on his trips, as with her lovely figure she is perfect to model his knitwear. Then, to my surprise, he tells me that he has rejoined the civil service, this time as a consultant to the Department of Foreign Affairs.

In this capacity I was instrumental in setting up a hand-knitting industry in a small country in southern Africa called Lesotho—one of the poorest countries in the world. Literally nobody there knew how to knit until I introduced the craft in 1980. I designed garments incorporating local motifs such as rondavels, aloe trees, crocodiles, etc., and now these garments which look and are indigenous are being knitted by hundreds of Lesotho women, and the monies earned as a result of the sales are of great benefit to many citizens of that poor country.

Dusk is beginning to fall, but before we begin our journey back to Dublin, we have one more treat in store for us; this has been a wonderful day of first experiences, but Cyril has kept the best for last.

It was perhaps inevitable that with his musical background, his children would inherit an interest in mastering musical instruments, an interest approved of by Cyril

Emily, Benita, Tara, and Margot Cullen playing their Irish harps.

and Margie, as they felt it would add another dimension to their lives. An old and rare harp standing in the drawing room encouraged the four girls to become harpists. Each has a harp of her own; they have appeared on several television shows, and played in many concerts not only in Ireland but also in England, France, and the United States. The two older girls, Emily and Benita, have been invited to perform at the Kennedy Center in Washington, D.C.

The Cullen sisters, with their exquisitely slim figures and straight long hair hanging to their waists, look like incarnations of the maidens we read about in early Irish literature. This impression was further endorsed when they began to play. As is their custom their first piece was "Sheebeg Sheemore" by O'Carolan. Then each girl played a solo. The finale literally brought tears to my eyes—the three older girls playing their harps accompanying the singing of the youngest, Margot.

Sitting in the beautiful Georgian drawing room with the fading light shining through the large eighteenth-century windows, and listening to the melodious strings of the harpists, we seemed to be suspended in time, belonging neither to the present nor the past.

Lacemaking

The English word "lace" owes something to the French lassis *or* lacis, *but both are derived from the earlier* Latin, laqueus  *(a noose).* Eventually, lace *referred to* ornamental open *work formed* with threads of *flax, cotton,* silk, gold, or silver, looped or braided or twisted together by hand, or with a point of a needle when the work is known as "needlepoint" lace, with bobbins, pins, and a pillow or cushion, when the lace is known as "pillow" lace. Lacemaking implied the production of ornament and fabric concurrently. Without a pattern or design the fabric of lace cannot be made. During the sixteenth century, or perhaps even earlier, lace was produced in many parts of Europe. The survival of a handsome antependium (a covering for the front of an altar), with the date 1641 I.D. (Isabel Dillon of Clonbrock) worked into the design, indicates that the technique was also known in Ireland. In fact, every known method of making lace by hand has at some time been practiced in Ireland. The earliest of these was bone lace, later known as bobbin or pillow lace. The publication of patterns for needlepoint and pillow lace dates from about the middle of the sixteenth century. From that time, stimulus to the industry in Europe was provided by regular trade demand together with the efforts of people like the teachers at the lace schools who

encouraged their pupils to spend their spare time learning to make lace which would give them a much-needed supplemental income. The origin and perpetuation of the craft became associated with the womenfolk of small farmers and fishermen, whether making lace in whitewashed cottages in rural Ireland, or those who produced lace during the eighteenth century along the lagoons of Venice, or Frenchwomen who made the sumptuous Points de France at Alençon and elsewhere in the eighteenth century. The ornamental character, however, of these laces would be found to differ greatly, but methods, materials, appliances, and opportunities of work would, in the main, be alike.

As wearing lace became fashionable, workers came to be drawn together into groups by employers who acted as channels for general trade. Nuns, in the past as in the present, have also devoted attention to the industry, often providing workrooms in the convent precincts not only for the rural women to carry out commissions in the service of the church or for trade but also for the purpose of training children in the craft. Elsewhere, lace schools had been founded by benefactors or organized by some leading local lacemaker, as much for trading as for education; in all this variety of circumstances, development of finer work has depended upon the abilities of the workers exercised under sound direction through their own intuitions, or supplied by intelligent and tasteful employers. Details of costumes in seventeenth-century

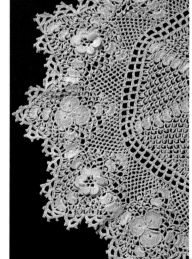

portraits illustrate how the early laces were used. It is an interesting point that both then and in the next century, men spent larger sums of money on lace than women.

King William of Orange is reputed to have paid nearly £2,500 for several items of lace in 1695; Queen Mary about £2,000 in 1694. Yet, compared with expenditure on lace at the French Court, these figures are insignificant.

In Ireland the Royal Dublin Society, ever ready to stimulate indigenous crafts, contributed grants from the society's general funds and Dr. Madden's special premiums (1743–1756) for individual performances. The records show claimants from all over the country, proving that lacemaking was widely practiced.

Early in the eighteenth century, Dean Swift had recognized the importance to Ireland of a flourishing lace industry in both economic and social terms. He encouraged Lady Arabella Denny to introduce lacemaking to the inmates of a Dublin orphanage, thus enabling fashionable people to buy home-produced goods instead of expensive imported European lace. This combination of philanthropy and patriotism, together with the active involvement of individuals, often with religious affiliations, was a pattern that remained unchanged for two hundred years. During the eighteenth and nineteenth centuries the wearing of lace centered around Dublin society. The special peak, however, must surely have been in 1907, a year best remembered for Lady Aberdeen's Vice-Regal ball at

Dublin Castle when even the men were required to wear some Irish lace—perhaps a jabot or an elaborate lace handkerchief.

The nineteenth century was the time when lacemaking in Ireland was at its most prosperous. Once trained, women and girls could execute the work at home while still being able to help with the farm work. Training in lacemaking was given free of charge at lace schools, a countrywide network of which sprang up in the middle and late years of the nineteenth century. Different areas were identified with different techniques, though in many cases more than one type of lace was produced in one place. A certain amount of confusion was caused by the association of place names with techniques; for instance, excellent lace using the Limerick technique was made at Newry, County Down, and the type of crochet referred to as Clones lace was also produced elsewhere.

The amount of training varied according to technique, from a few weeks for basic crochet to many years in the case of needlepoint. As a result the quantities produced and relative costs of different laces varied, as did their uses. The most expensive laces were generally used by the Church and on State occasions. Most of the designs executed were copies of European lace. However, where technical understanding and artistry were combined, exquisite results were achieved, and a book of beautiful designs executed by two of the Poor Clare nuns for Kenmare point lace, often for British and European royalty, can still be seen at the Poor Clare convent at Kenmare.

Different sources of influence were involved in lacemaking in Ireland. Carrick macross lace evolved from a piece of appliqué lace which the wife of the Reverend John Grey Porter, Rector of Donaghmoyne, County Monaghan, brought back from Italy in 1816. Appliqué work was already known and practiced, but applications of cambric patterns to net, and further embellishment with point stitches, was new and original. At first Mrs. Porter and her gifted sewing maid, Ann Steadman, were merely interested in lacework. However, in 1820 agriculture and trade in Ireland were so depressed that they started appliqué classes. These were successful and many women and girls soon become quite expert and the method spread to other schools. Anxious to ease conditions after the Famine of 1848, Captain Morant, agent of the Shirley estate, turned a vacant house in Carrickmacross into a lace school, and no fewer than seven branch schools were erected on the estate. From the central school, designs, instructions, and orders were distributed, and for many years a succession of good teachers ensured the quality of the products. The lace received its official name Carrickmacross Lace at the Dublin exhibition of 1872.

Toward the end of the nineteenth century, the lace industry was again in danger, some schools had closed and standards of work degenerated, which caused the market to decline. The position was saved when the nuns of the St. Louis Convent came to Carrickmacross in 1888. They taught lacemaking in their schools and obtained good new designs, at the same time making sure that promising workers knew enough about drawing to adapt patterns to suit customers' needs. The survival of Carrickmacross lace well into this century is due to the efforts of the St. Louis nuns.

In the sixties, seventies, and early eighties of this century, lace reached its most fashionable peak. Wedding gowns and veils, evening and cocktail dresses and blouses were made of Carrickmacross lace, and were worn by some of the most famous and elegant women in the world, many of whom have since donated their lace dresses to costume museums across several continents. In the eighties there was a falling-off of vocations to the religious life, and as the nuns who were involved with the lacemaking grew old, and in some cases died, once again Carrickmacross lace went into decline.

But this was not to be the end of the story.

Kenmare Lace

On the evening of October 24, 1861, a long car driven by three horses arrived at the County Kerry town of Kenmare. Appropriately it was the feast of the Archangel, Saint Raphael, the patron of travelers. The occupants of the car were seven nuns of the Order of Saint Clare, known as the Poor Clares, and Archdeacon John O'Sullivan—Father John, as he was affectionately referred to.

For some time past, he had been anxious to provide for the educational needs of his people. In consultation with the bishop, it was agreed that they would invite the Poor Clare nuns in Newry to send a small group of their sisters to Kenmare, as a foundation for a convent school. The seven nuns came from different parts of Ireland; their leader was the Mother Abbess of the Newry Convent, Mother Michael O'Hagan. This saintly and talented woman regarded the invitation to Kenmare as a call from God. In time she would become celebrated as the Nun of Kenmare.

The new convent was in the process of being built, so for almost a year the sisters lived in uncomfortable and cramped conditions in Rose Cottage, which adjoined the church grounds; the lectures themselves were held in a large timber yard. The nuns faced a formidable task; they had left well-ordered schools in a large, comparatively prosperous town and were now called upon to establish a new school for a wide and remote area of great poverty and depression. The local people were only gradually recovering from the general paralysis caused by the Famine. Some five thousand had died in the year 1846 alone; two years later more than ten thousand people were still receiving outdoor relief. It is little wonder that Father John rejoiced to have secured the services of nuns whose special vocation was to the poor, in the spirit of their founders, Saint Francis of Assisi and Saint Clare.

From the beginning the poor were the nuns' first priority; they fed and clothed them, they comforted them in their afflictions, and they taught the children.

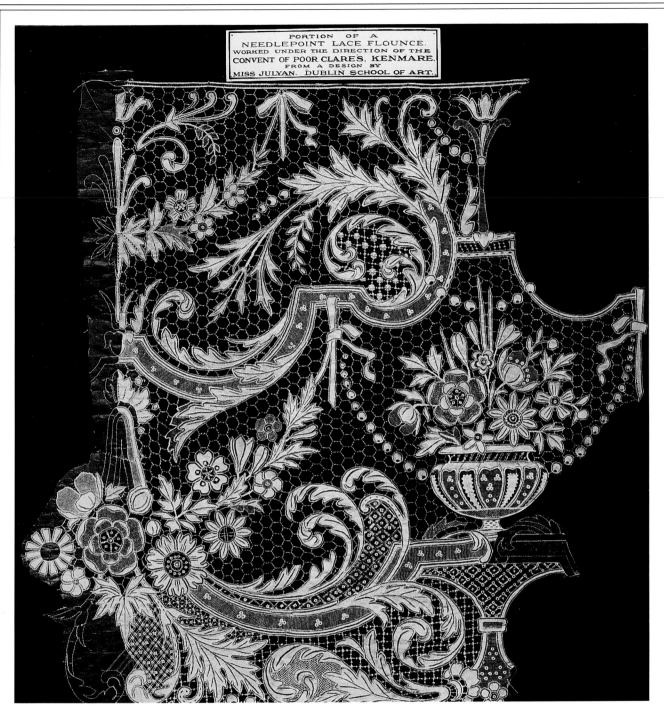

Unfinished fichu of Kenmare lace, thought to be the prize-winning piece which Queen Victoria ordered for her personal use.

Many of the children, in their eagerness to learn, came long distances; even in the depths of winter they defied the severest weather, very often tramping barefoot for miles down the mountain gorges, and through rapid rivers. They had no woollen garments—their clothes were of the flimsiest kind.

It is clear from official records that the education given to the children in the convent school was of an exceptionally high standard. As the years progressed the school entered upon a long and golden era during which to have been educated by the Poor Clare Convent in Kenmare was accepted as a hallmark of training and refinement.

After the Great Famine, Father John had opened a crochet lace school in Kenmare to give employment to women and girls in an effort to alleviate their poverty. At the arrival of the nuns, Mother O'Hagan took over the running of the lace school. In the late sixties she procured a good teacher from the Presentation Convent in Youghal where the workers had been making needlepoint lace for several years.

In the year 1869 needlepoint lace began to be made at Kenmare. Although other centers of lacemaking occasionally used other threads, linen thread was used exclusively in Kenmare. Several types of needlepoint were produced at Kenmare; appliqué and guipure were also taught. What made Kenmare unique was that it was made entirely with a needle and thread, without inset of pieces of fabric, and without a supporting net mesh.

Soon Kenmare lace began to gain a high reputation for design and execution. Samples of the lace were entered in competitions both in Ireland and in Great Britain, and were the recipient of many prizes. In the year 1886 the Department of Science and Art at South Kensington, London, sent over a lace expert, Alan Cole, C.B., to give illustrated lectures at the various lace schools throughout Ireland. The local newspaper, *The Kerry Sentinel*, quoted Mr. Cole thus:

At Kenmare instruction is given in both elementary drawing and designing. Within the comparatively short time since the class was formed the influence of better drawing and arrangement in the designs worked by the school of lace-workers here has been felt.

Mr. Cole then went on to make reference to Kenmare's most prestigious customer:

Her Majesty, Queen Victoria, who had graciously taken notice of the progress of the movement from its commencement, was pleased to sanction the execution of specimen laces from five of the prize designs, . . . one of them by a member of the community of Poor Clares at Kenmare. The prize design was a charming fichu of needlepoint lace.

In November 1886 Mr. Cole again visited the lace school at Kenmare and recorded the following comment:

I inspected various designs made by the nuns. Of these the largest and probably the most important ever made for Irish lace work is that of a quilt and cover for pillows, to execute which in needlepoint lace the nuns have received a commission. The quilt is about nine feet six inches square and the pillow cover about five feet two inches by three feet three inches.

This quilt was designed for a Mrs. Winnace, the wife of an American millionaire. It sold for a staggering £300 in the year 1886.

Many medals were secured by Kenmare lace over the following years. King Edward VII followed the example of his mother when he patronized the lace school at Kenmare in the year 1903, purchasing a collarette of magnificent needlepoint for Queen Alexandra for the modest sum of £12. At the National Gallery in Washington, D.C., there is a wall hanging of Kenmare needlepoint lace depicting Eire with the traditional round tower and wolfhound motifs.

Among the wedding gifts received by Queen Elizabeth II of England was a bedcover of antique Kenmare lace.

The art of Kenmare needlepoint was for a long time a forgotten art, but happily it was revived in recent years under the direction of Sisters Frances and Leontia, the only two members of the community who still know how to master the intricacies of this most exquisite of Irish laces.

Clones Lace

Crochet or Clones lace is probably the best known of all Irish laces. Its character and quality vary greatly according to place and time of production. It was introduced by the nuns of the Ursuline Convent at Blackrock, County Cork, through the influence of a local gentlewoman, Honoria Nagle. It is not dissimilar to ordinary crochet except for its fineness. The best work of the past was produced using a hook and thread of the same thickness; hooks were sometimes made by removing one side of the eye of an ordinary needle, sewing, and sticking the point in a cork. The design is drawn on glazed calico, the motif is worked individually and then tacked into place on the calico. They are joined together with crochet chainstitch and the backing removed when all the motifs have been sewn.

In 1847 Thomas Hand was appointed Rector of the Church of Ireland in Clones, County Monaghan. His English wife, Cassandra, was struck by

the poor living conditions of the people in the area, caused, in the main, by the potato famine. She resolved to bring to Clones teachers to instruct the local women and girls in the craft of lacemaking. At first they used samples of Valenciennes and Point lace as examples. So proficient did they become that the Clones lacemakers not only learned to copy the imported motifs but were soon devising ones of their own.

Like all artists they were inspired by things they saw around them—the fern, the cockscomb, the thistle, the wheel, the scroll, and, of course, the rose and shamrock. Sometimes families devised their special motifs, which were handed down from mother to daughter. It was their signature on the work, and those familiar with the local lace could easily identify the maker. A distinctive joining stitch was also developed, which marked the lace as coming from Clones.

*Rose and shamrock Clones lace table mat chosen by
H.R.H. Princess Anne as her wedding gift from
the people of Ulster.*

This was a rolled dot which gave the lace a very rich look; it was called the Clones knot.

The teaching of the craft was so successful that at one time between the areas of County Monathan and South Armagh there were fifteen hundred lacemakers in the area; they were mostly women and children, but some men and boys. One of the privileges accorded to the lacemakers in farm families was that they were excused from milking the cows, as this tended to roughen their hands.

Cassandra Hand used her contacts with the gentry to promote the lace for fashiona-

ble wear, household adornment, and church use. Markets were developed at home and abroad, and soon Clones lace was being sold all over Europe as well as in the United States. In the early 1900s Isobel, Marchioness of Aberdeen, came to Ireland as wife of the Viceroy. She became an ardent supporter of the cottage crafts, in particular handwoven tweeds and handmade lace; she devoted herself to their promotion.

The Lace Ball, inaugurated by her, was an annual highlight of the Social Calendar. Men and women alike were expected to wear lace. On one occasion, when Isobel was ill, rather than miss the ball, she arrived in a wheelchair, dressed entirely in handmade Irish lace.

Maire Connolly crocheting Clones lace. Collar and skirt of Clones lace.

Skirt of peacock-blue Irish poplin worn with blouse of pleated Irish linen, trimmed with hand crocheted lace.

Around 1910 the lace industry began to go into decline; lace was not as fashionable as it had been hitherto, and less expensive machine-made lace became available. The year 1914 saw the beginning of the First World War; jobs in munition factories paid wages far and above any amount that women could earn from long hours of craftwork. However, the tradition of lacemaking did not completely die out in the area; it continued as a cottage industry right up to the years after the Second World War.

Two sisters, the Misses Gunn, working with a small group of women, living near the village of Five-mile-town in County Tyrone, had for many years supplied the linen for the households of the British Royal Family.

When Her Royal Highness, Princess Anne (now the Princess Royal), was being married, the citizens of Ulster wanted to give her a wedding present that was indigenous to northern Ireland. They contacted the Misses Gunn and the princess chose a set of place mats made of Clones lace, using the rose and shamrock motifs.

As a wedding present for His Royal Highness, the Prince of Wales, and Lady Diana Spencer, the royal couple chose a set of place mats and napkins of Irish linen embellished with a wide border of Clones lace in the wheel design which included the famous Clones knot. These also were made by the Misses Gunn's team of workers.

Today, when people talk about Clones lace, they talk about Mamo McDonald, who, like Sister Enda and Martha Hughes, is fighting to revive the most famous of the area's crafts. A Clones Lace Guild has been formed; an exhibition of antique lace was held at Mamo McDonald's premises to mark County Monaghan's Heritage Year; it attracted not only local interest but also that of tourists from China, Japan, the United States, Canada, Australia, and many European countries. A young Japanese woman spent many weeks in Clones recently learning lacemaking. She reached a high level of skill, and intends to teach it in Japan.

The Cassandra Hand Summer School of Clones Lace has just been started. Mamo McDonald is devoting all her considerable energies to making it a success.

The craft of lacemaking has always been associated with women, and many of them had religious connections—Mother Michael O'Hagan of Kenmare, the Sisters of St. Louis Convent, Carrickmacross, Cassandra Hand, wife of the Church of Ireland Rector in Clones, to name a few. In fact the story of the Irish lace industry is the story of the women of Ireland, and it is as relevant today as it was in the eighteenth and nineteenth centuries.

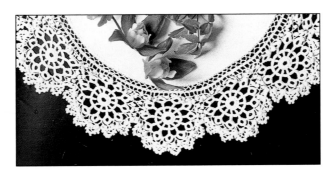

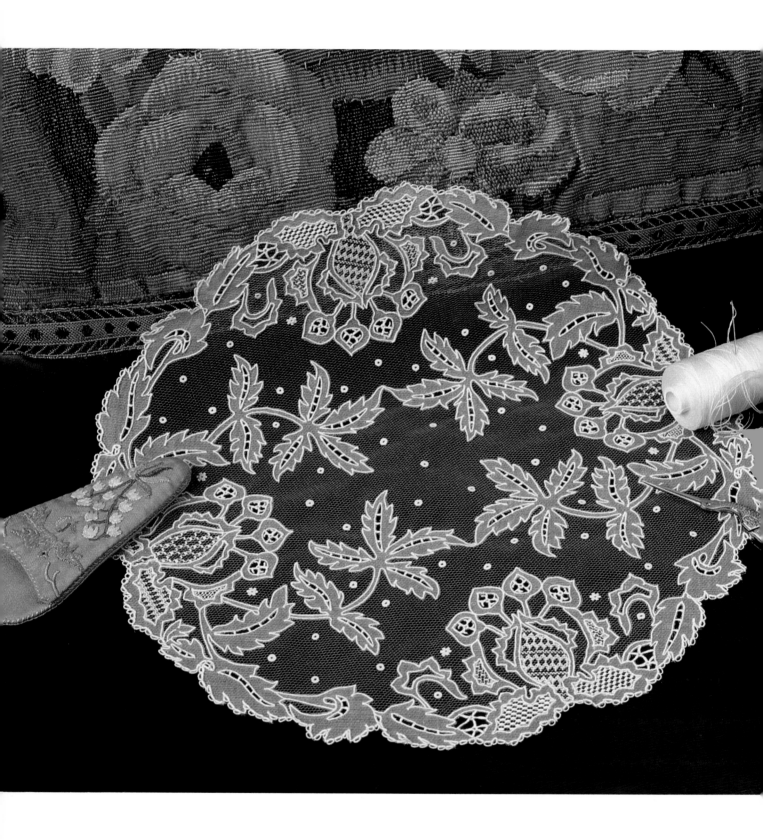

Martha Hughes and Sister Enda
Carrickmacross Lace

On a clear sunny morning in June I set out for Carrickmacross, County Monaghan, a medium-size town about fifty miles north of Dublin, which in the nineteenth century gave its name to one of the most beautiful handmade laces. For the past ten years the making of the lace had been in something of a decline. Rumors of a spirited revival in the making of Carrickmacross lace had reached my ears. As a couturiere, I had in the past used it extensively in my collections, and had lamented its demise, so this journey was one of hope as well as curiosity. An early start had insured an almost traffic-free road.

Nothing could be more joyful than a blue sky hanging over a glorious panorama of golden brown and green fields, a landscape of gentle undulations, harmonious and benign. The dense foliage of the hedgerows was decked out in billows of pale pink dog roses and sweetly scented elders, the latter looking like an alley of cream lace parasols. Red poppies were out in the cornfields and oxeye

daisies that were recently nodding on bare banks were now almost buried in tall grass.

Released from the confines of the city, it is as though one had escaped into a long-lost pastoral golden age when summers were synonymous with the smell of new-mown hay and the scent of honey issuing from a field of clover. Altogether it seemed a way of verifying that the excitement felt during childhood summers was not an illusion after all.

Out of the corner of my eye I saw a hazy blue vision gleaming like a sapphire in the fold of a hill and realized it was one of the many lakes for which County Monaghan is famous.

It must have been at least ten years since my last visit to Carrickmacross. Driving into the town the first reaction is one of pleasure—it is obvious that here is a place with a strong community spirit, for pavements are lined with large containers planted with white petunias and red geraniums. The streets are clean and tidy, and shopfronts look freshly painted, their windows inviting. My appointment with Martha Hughes was at the Lace Gallery at the end of the main street. It is well-posted; I had no trouble finding it and Martha Hughes, long-limbed and elegant, was sitting there waiting for me. We didn't waste time, so over coffee she told me her story that is inexorably linked with the revival of Carrickmacross lace.

My husband, Martin, and I were born in County Mayo. In 1974 we came to live in Carrickmacross. I am naturally curious, so straight away I set about learning the attractions of our adopted country.

I learned that within a ten-mile radius of the town there are no fewer than forty lakes, justifying its claim to be Ireland's finest coarse-fishing center, but undoubtedly the town's longest and greatest fame is that it is the home of the handmade lace which, since the middle of the nineteenth century, bears its name.

Sister Enda is art teacher at the Convent School of the St. Louis nuns; lacemaking is taught as a subject on the curriculum. The more I was exposed to the lace, the more determined I became to learn its techniques.

There are two methods for making Carrickmacross lace—appliqué and guipure. Appliqué is done by tacking fine net over a design drawn on paper. On top of this is placed a layer of muslin. The design is then outlined by sewing through both layers of the fabric with a thick thread sewn down at close intervals with a fine one. The surplus muslin is then cut away and filling stitches, of the type used in Limerick lace, are added. The character of Carrickmacross ap-

pliqué made today differs from older lace because of the change in available materials. Net with hexagonal mesh has replaced soft cotton bobbin net, and organza is used instead of muslin. Guipure is made without a ground or mesh; the pattern is held in place by threads.

"Was learning how to make the lace very difficult?" I ask Martha.

Yes it was, for as a beginner you receive gentle encouragement linked to a quiet despair at your clumsiness. They tell you soothingly that all you need to succeed is time and patience. Not true. You need superhuman vigilance, laser vision, and surgical precision. You have to learn a whole new language, words like loops, pips, filling-in stitches—for example, diamond, cobweb, double dot, daisy, thorns, and bars, these are constantly on your lips during the day, and in your dreams at night. But somehow one perseveres and the day dawns when you realize that overcoming all obstacles you have mastered the art of making Carrickmacross lace.

In the course of my lessons, I met people who, like me, marveled at the beauty of the craft, and were anxious to revive it, in order to share its qualities with a wider audience.

A committee was formed with a view to setting up a cooperative movement. This came into being in 1984. In 1990 I was elected chairperson of the movement. A long-held ambition was to have a showcase for the public to view the lace. We succeeded in obtaining these premises, and it is here that the proud tradition of the skills of the Carrickmacross laceworker is displayed and sold.

At that moment we are joined by Sister Enda herself. She is as pretty as a picture,

Designs for parasol covers made of Carrickmacross lace.

Sister Enda of the St. Louis Order designing a pattern for a Carrickmacross lace collar.

with black curly hair and smiling eyes. About her is an aura of a woman at ease with herself. I ask her to tell me about her life and how she came to be involved with the revival of lacemaking at Carrickmacross.

I was born and grew up in Glenariffe, the loveliest of the Glens of Antrim, so from my earliest childhood I was surrounded by, and enthralled with, landscapes and seascapes of extraordinary beauty. It was perhaps therefore inevitable that I would have been drawn into a lifelong exploration of beauty which finds expression in my combined love of art and spirituality.

Carrickmacross lace christening robe, awarded first prize by the Royal Dublin Society.

I was educated at the St. Louis Convent School, Ballymena, and subsequently became a St. Louis sister. After graduating from Belfast College of Art and Design, I was appointed art teacher at the St. Louis Secondary School, Carrickmacross.

As a first-year project in college, I had researched Carrickmacross lace. At that time the administrator at the St. Louis Lace Centre was Sister Laurence, and it was she who taught me the basic techniques of lace; this training from a woman who had a lifelong commitment to and expertise in lacemaking stood me in good stead when I was first asked to design a commissioned piece. This first commission, nearly twenty years ago, was for the President of Ireland's rail *coach. It was to be the forerunner of many commissions.*

Our sisters of the St. Louis Convent had developed a partnership with local groups; when the Carrickmacross Lace Co-operative was established in 1984, rather than have a duplication of services, the Sisters decided to close the St. Louis lace center, and instead, to support the co-operative.

Martha feels that apart from its more obvious advantages the Lace Gallery serves as an influence and incentive to the local people to continue making this valuable craft. Many of the pieces on display were designed by Sister Enda. A glorious collar of lace, designed by her and worked by Martha, in 1990 won an award at the National Craft competition at the Royal Dublin Society. The National Museum is interested in obtaining this collar for its permanent collection.

In 1992 Martha again was a winner of the above award, this time for her work on a christening robe, also designed by Sister Enda. At present as part of the cooperative movement, there are twenty-five workers making lace to fulfill orders. In the winter months Martha gives lessons in lace-making.

Her time is given voluntarily, but she maintains that it has brought her a great deal of satisfaction, which, when one sees the quality of the work, is totally understandable.

During our conversation we had been interrupted several times by people, mostly tourists, who, learning of the existence of the Lace Gallery, had come to see the samples which are displayed in glass-front showcases. Glancing at the visitors' book I see that on the previous day, people of fourteen different nationalities had signed their names.

In the capable hands of Martha Hughes and Sister Enda, the new era of Carrickmacross lace is going to be long-lived and successful.

Irish Linen

Linen is a natural fiber indigenous to western Europe, and comes from the flax plant, Linum usitatissimum. From the earliest  periods of human history until the beginning of the nineteenth century, the manufacture of linen was one of the most extensive and widely dispersed of the domestic industries in Europe. The industry was largely developed in Russia, Austria, Germany, Belgium, Holland, the northern provinces of France, the north of Ireland, and throughout Scotland, and in these countries its importance was generally recognized by the enactment of special laws having for their object the protection and extension of the trade.

In England the linen industry was always overshadowed by

the wool trade and has never commanded the respect accorded

to Irish linen. Flax was probably grown in Ireland from

the early Bronze Age onward. There are many mentions

of flax and linen 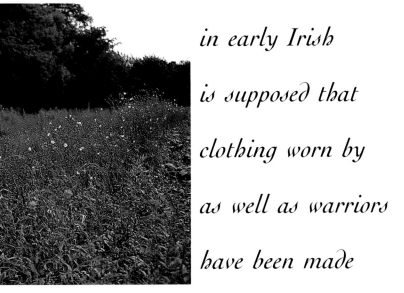 in early Irish

literature, and it is supposed that

the descriptions of clothing worn by

kings and queens, as well as warriors

and maidens, would have been made

from either wool or linen. By tradition, flax-seed should be

sown on Saint Patrick's Day, March 17, but this date has

been moved to mid-April when the weather is more clement.

Flax is a high-yielding plant and until the mid-eighteenth

century, the cultivation of flax and the making of linen

Blouse of finely pleated linen with pewter gray linen skirt,
hand embroidered with Georgian-inspired motifs.

was widespread, with each household growing its own. Processing the flax and spinning the thread was done exclusively by women, and gave rise to the term "spinster."

The preparation of flax for spinning has varied little over the centuries, the flax is harvested (nowadays by machine where once it was pulled from the ground by hand in order to preserve the maximum length of the fibers), it is then put into bunches which are stooked (stood on end), to allow the seed heads to dry and ripen. The dry seed heads are removed by passing the tips of the stalks through a coarse comb, called a ripple, then they are gathered and crushed for linseed oil or cattle feed. The most important stage, retting, or separating the fibers from the rest of the stem, comes next. In the old days the flax was spread outside over grass and left from four to seven weeks to allow the dew, sun, and rain to rot the binding and free the fibers. The flax is dried again before it is scutched, that is, beaten to break any fibers which might be left. Finally it is hackled—pulled through a comb of nails several times to remove any remaining straw and short fibers—and then it is ready to be spun into linen yarn.

Present-day methods of spinning flax remain similar to those used in earlier times. Linen has no elasticity, and as it is strong even when wet, it is essential to keep it moist when weaving; some weavers coat the warp with a weak solution of Polycell or wallpaper paste to prevent fraying and breaking. When linen comes off the loom it is stiff and coarse, so it has to be boiled in soapy water for about an hour to soften the cloth before being partially bleached. This is called grassing or crofting. In the past, warps of fabric were laid out on grass and exposed to the elements until the desired degree of whiteness was obtained.

Linen as a fabric has several advantages over cotton, principally due to the microscopic structure and length of the flax fibers. The cloth is much smoother and more lustrous than cotton cloth and presents a less "woolly" surface so it does not soil as readily or absorb and retain moisture as freely as the more spongy cotton; and it is at once a cool, clean, and healthy material for bedsheets and clothing. Flax is a slightly heavier material than cotton, while its strength is about double.

For more than three hundred years the province of Ulster, in northern Ireland, has been the chief linen-producing region in these islands. The prosperity of the Irish linen industry depended on its exports. Trade followed the flag throughout the British Empire in the nineteenth century, and in cooperation with merchants of many countries, Irish linen became known throughout the world. This success was founded on a resolve to produce the highest quality linens, and a genuine appreciation of the properties of linen that was translated into fine cloth, notably damask and cambric. The industry generated several important ancillary crafts such as embroidery, hemstitching, and shirtmaking that employed many thousands of women throughout Ulster and enhanced the value of linen production.

Because the climate in Ireland was conducive to growing good quality flax, weavers remained independent craftsmen throughout much of the eighteenth cen-

Hand-embroidered Irish linen hand towels inherited
from the author's grandmother.

tury, and many became sufficiently affluent to lease small holdings convenient to major markets. The great number of farmer-weavers left a permanent impression on the social structure of Ulster. In the long run, however, the greatest profits were earned in the finishing processes by those bleachers who managed to reduce their bleaching costs by installing water-driven machinery and adopting chemical bleaching. They became the capitalists of the industry, and were responsible in the following century for managing its transition from the cottage to the factory.

Among the crafts generated by the linen industry was the printing and dyeing of patterns on cloth. This craft had established itself in Dublin around 1745 to supply the fashionable market there.

In the 1950s the linen industry had recovered after the Second World War to employ 55,000 people, and there were four hundred mills, factories, and plants connected with Irish linen production. More than 90 percent of its production was exported. However, there were great changes happening in textiles throughout the world. Linen was being challenged by other materials in a market that was becoming more conscious of color and design, while demanding immediate availability at increasingly low prices. Linen had long faced competition from cotton, especially in bed linens. When handkerchiefs, napkins, place mats, and hand towels made from paper were introduced, linen couldn't compete.

Then, in the early fifties, almost overnight, Irish linen became a high-fashion fabric. The covers and inside pages of the top fashion publications began to show beautiful pictures of romantic evening dresses made from finely pleated (or crushed) Irish linen. In fact, the seeds of this renaissance had been sown almost two years earlier in the Belfast showrooms of the linen firm of Spence Bryson.

As a couturiere, I was forever bemoaning the fact that it was well-nigh impossible to find Irish linen fine enough to use for evening gowns. It suddenly occurred to me that Spence Bryson, among other things, made the finest handkerchiefs for the luxury market, their justifiably proud boast being that they made the handkerchiefs for the "kings of Europe." (In the early fifties there were many more ruling kings in Europe than there are today.) At my request exquisitely fine linens were brought for my inspection and I knew immediately that I had found what I was looking for. However, there was one serious disadvantage to using this material for apparel, for it was pointed out to me that linen of this fine quality would disintegrate if put through a crease-resisting process.

Being something of a Doubting Thomas, I squeezed the linen in my hand to see just how badly it would crush, and I had to admit that, in its present state, it would be impossible to use for my intended purpose.

But a challenge invariably makes one creative; after pondering the question for some time, and in conjunction with the workroom staff, it was decided to experiment to see if we could develop a process that would permanently crush, or pleat, the linen, and so make a feature of the problem, rather than an insurmountable drawback. It took eight months, during which time we put many theories to the test, be-

Finely pleated Irish linen skirt with hand-crocheted Irish lace blouse, photographed in the Great Banqueting hall of Bunratty Castle.

fore we came up with the correct solution.

The process we decided upon still remains our secret.

As the linen is handkerchief linen, it is prepared to be white in color, but the mill had it dyed to the colors of my choosing, gorse yellow, peat brown, purple (for this color a petal was taken from a clematis in the garden, put into an envelope and sent to Spence Bryson), apricot, pink, sky blue—there is hardly a color we have not experimented with.

When a client decides on a style, the crushed linen is pinned, sometimes with as many as a thousand pins, to a base of either taffeta or silk before it is sewn. The linen is then cut to the model chosen by the client. Nine yards pleats into one yard, so in each dress there are about sixty to seventy yards of linen. As the material is as fine as a spider web, despite the number of yards, there is no sense of weight. An added bonus is, that having been exposed to our process, the entire gown is crease-resistant.

The first dress we made from the pleated linen was an evening gown, appropriately called First Love. It was included in a fashion show at the Plaza Hotel in New York City that showed models from Paris, Milan, and London. The fashion press, always on the lookout for something new, wrote ecstatically about First Love and its fabric. A new era for Irish linen had begun.

In the early 1980s Italian designers became enamored with Irish linen. The world had become conscious of mankind's damage to the environment and as part of this awareness natural fibers were very much to the fore.

While the linen industry throughout the world contracted in the face of competition from synthetic fibers, one has to pay tribute to the tenacity and resilience of an industry that has been able to respond so well to a world of new opportunities. Irish linen has been in existence for three hundred years, and although reduced in number today, the linen industry will be around for a long time to come.

Printed Textiles

Textile, a general name given to all woven fabrics, comes from the Latin texere, to weave. The art of ornamenting such fabrics by printing on designs or patterns in color is very ancient, probably originating in the East. It has been practiced in some form with considerable success in China and India from time immemorial, and the Chinese at least are known to have made use of engraved woodblocks many centuries before any kind of printing was known in Europe. That the early Egyptians too were acquainted with the art is proved, not merely by the writings of Pliny the Elder, but by the discovery, in the Pyramids and other Egyptian tombs, of fragments of cloth which were certainly decorated by some method of printing. There is no doubt that India was the source from which, through two different channels, Europeans derived their knowledge of block-printing. By land its practice spread westward through Persia, Asia Minor, and the Levant, until it was taken up in Europe during the latter half of the seventeenth century. Almost at the same time the French brought directly by sea, from their colonies on the east coast of India, samples of India blue and white "resist" prints, and with them, particulars of the process by which they had been produced. Textile printing was introduced into England in 1676 by a French refugee who opened works, in that year, on the bank of the Thames near Richmond. It was in 1738 that calico printing was first practiced in Scotland, and not until twenty-six years later that Messrs Clayton, at Bamber Bridge, near Preston, established in 1764 the first printed works in Lancashire, and thus laid the foundation of what was to become one of the most important industries in that country. However, the production of the French printers in Jouy, Beauvais, Rouen, etc., was generally regarded as "all that was best" in artistic calico printing. But in one respect a printing firm in Dublin was ahead of all others.

On October 3, 1752, an advertisement appeared in *Faulkner's Journal* stating that "Drumcondra printed linens, done from metal plates (a method never before practised), with all the advantages of light and shade in the strongest and most lasting colours" could be bought from George Gibbens at the Hen and Chicken in Werburgh Street, Dublin. These printed stuffs, described two months later by Mrs. Delany, the diarist and maker of flower mosaics, as being "excessively pretty" were made by Francis Nixon.

Until Nixon's process, linens or fustian (linen warp and cotton weft) were printed using woodblocks. Engraved copperplates were used only for such items as commemorative handkerchiefs, as the dyes suitable for copperplate printing could not be made colorfast to soap and water. Cotton fabric could not be used until 1774 when the English government's prohibition on pure cotton, imposed by the silk and wool industry to counter the popularity of imported Indian cotton chintzes, was lifted.

Nixon refined the mordants used with natural madder and indigo dyes to make it possible to print with a single color using engraved copperplates, thus introducing finer, more delicate draftsmanship with high definition and far larger repeats—over a yard square—than was possible using woodblocks, which were only one foot square. Madder, for shades of pink, red, and purple, and indigo for China blue were used.

Nixon soon realized the commercial potential of his new technique, and so, when a wealthy East India merchant, George Amyand, M.P. for Barnstable, approached him, he did not hesitate to sell the technique to him. Amyand promptly set Nixon up in a new print works at Phippsbridge, near Merton, Surrey, around 1757.

Throughout the 1760s Irish and English manufacturers produced stuff printed with elegant pictorial designs—chinoiseries, flowers and birds, pastoral and mythological scenes often based on etchings and engravings by well-known artists. Some firms were producing designs with repeats six feet high. Talwin and Foster's works at Bromley Hall on the River Lea produced designs of such quality that it is only since the result of pioneering researches at the Victoria and Albert Museum in the 1950s that they have been identified as English, and not attributed to the Jouy factory in France. Several Dublin firms, such as Robinsons of Ballsbridge, also used Nixon's process. Robinson had been one of the many craftspeople given financial assistance by the Royal Dublin Society. An exquisite printed cotton designed by him, featuring architectural columns, exotic birds and animals, human figures, and a cornucopia of flowers and fruits is in the collection of the National Museum of Ireland. In 1988 permission was given to have the design reprinted, perhaps for the first time in more than two hundred years, for use in the decoration of a restored Cottage Ornée (referred to as the Swiss Cottage in Ireland), in Cahir, County Tipperary, reputedly designed by John Nash in 1810.

When Marie Antoinette chose new bed hangings from the Jouy factory, she covered every surface with toile—bed hangings, curtains, chair upholstery, even walls, cupboards, and doors would all be covered in fabric as though enclosing oneself in an imaginary world of mythological scenes or idealized rural life.

Early in the twentieth century wallpaper manufacturers began to reproduce many of the earlier designs for toile. The fabrics have been constantly reproduced, sometimes using the original techniques and colors.

Today Glendennings, Lurgan, northern Ireland, is perhaps the most successful printing firm in Ireland.

Precious Metals

Gold

Silver

Gold

Gold is a metallic chemical element, valued from earliest times on account of the permanency of its color and luster. When pure it is the most malleable of all metals; a single  grain may be drawn into a wire fifty feet in length, and an ounce of gold covering a silver wire is capable of being extended more than fourteen hundred yards. Gold forms alloys with most metals, and of these many are of great importance to the arts. In ancient literature gold is the universal symbol of the highest purity and value. Gold ornaments of great variety and elaborate workmanship have been discovered on sites belonging to the earliest known civilizations—Minoan, Egyptian, Assyrian, Etruscan, and

Cretan. Archaeological excavations during the past twenty-

five years at Thessaloníki, capital of Macedonia, have

unearthed treasures of

exquisite workmanship and

design, ascribed to the fourth

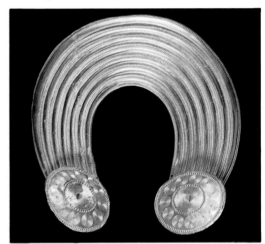

century B.C. The supply

of gold, and also its relation to the supply of silver, has,

among civilized nations, always been of paramount impor-

tance to the economic questions concern-

ing money.

It is known that during the Bronze

Age a large quantity of gold was

available in Ireland. Although gold has

The Ardagh chalice, eighth century A.D. *(left) and the Derrynaflan chalice, ninth century* A.D. *(right). The chalice on the right was discovered in 1980.*

been found here at a number of locations, particularly in County Wicklow and County Tyrone, the earliest sources have still to be identified; they would have been alluvial deposits from rivers and streams. Perhaps the sites were exploited by prehistoric people.

In Europe the earliest evidence of goldworking dates to 5000 B.C. By the end of the third millennium the working of gold, as well as copper and bronze, had been well established in both Ireland and Britain. One can only speculate as to how the late Neolithic people of Ireland became familiar with metalworking, but it would appear that it was introduced as a fully developed craft by people already experienced at all levels of production from identification and recovery through the various stages of the goldworking process.

The Celts arrived in Ireland about 500 to 600 B.C. They brought with them a comparatively sophisticated structure of government and a knowledge of crafts, metalwork in particular. They had an extraordinary feeling for nature and this is reflected in their artifacts.

Little is known for sure about the Celts. They were first glimpsed around the sixth century B.C., and over the next five centuries they expanded to Britain and Ireland as well as other European countries.

During the early Bronze Age (between 2200 to 1700 B.C.) the goldsmiths produced a small range of ornaments, sun disks, plain and decorated, and, most important, the crescentic gold collars called lunulae (Latin for "little moon"). These pieces were all made from sheet gold, a technique well demonstrated by the lunulae, many of which were beaten out extremely thin. Geometric motifs such as lozenges, triangles, and groups of lines arranged in patterns were used for decoration, as well as incisions, using a sharp tool, and repoussé (working from behind to produce a raised pattern).

Around 1200 B.C. new gold techniques must have been developed because there was a distinct change in the types of ornaments produced in the workshops. Twisting bars of gold became the method most commonly used for a variety of objects ranging from earrings to waist torques. In particular, the latter required the use of large amounts of gold, so it is reasonable to assume that a new source of the metal had been discovered.

The period between 1000 and 850 B.C. was curiously devoid of evidence of gold-working, but difficulty in identifying objects of this period may account for the apparent gap. The succeeding phase is noted for the great variety and quality of both gold and bronze working.

By now the goldsmiths had developed to a very high degree all the skills necessary to make a large range of ornaments, using many techniques and forms of decoration. Bracelets, dress fasteners, and neck rings made from bars and ingots were produced, as were the more delicate collars, boxes, and disks made from sheet gold. Thin gold foil, sometimes heavily decorated, was used to cover items made from other metals.

Our knowledge of Bronze Age goldwork from Ireland is based to a large degree on the discovery of groups of objects found in hoards. As many as 160 hoards of the Late Bronze Age have come to light in Ireland. They have been found in the course of turf-cutting, plowing, and quarrying. It is seldom that they are found during archaeological excavations because the places in which they were deposited are remote from settlements and burial sites, which might suggest that the hoards were hidden during a time of siege, or stress of some kind.

The contents of hoards vary considerably; they may consist of a mixture of tools, weapons, and personal ornaments, or they may contain a single object; others have included a mixture of gold and bronze pieces, and sometimes necklaces of amber beads. A large hoard of gold ornaments found close

to a lake in Mooghaun, north County Clare, in 1854 contained over 150 objects, consisting mostly of bracelets, but also six gold collars and two neck rings. A large proportion of the gold objects made during the Early and Late Bronze ages were for personal adornment.

The most beautiful piece of early gold in the National Museum is the fragile almost paper-thin golden boat, with its exquisite fine oars, mast, and rudder. It dates from the Iron Age 100 B.C. On a February evening in 1896, Thomas Nicholl of Broighter, County Derry, northern Ireland, was double-ploughing a stubble field to a depth of eleven inches, when he came up against an obstruction. Closer inspection revealed a number of metal objects; it didn't occur to him that they might be gold. The boat was only one item in what became known as the Broighter hoard. Next day they were sold to a Derry jeweler, then to a Cork antiquarian, Robert Day, who had the objects restored and sold them to the British Museum for £600. Meanwhile, the Royal Irish Academy had declared that the objects should be "treasure trove" and returned to Ireland. A legal battle ensued, and eventually the hoard was handed over to King Edward VII, who gave it to the Royal Irish Academy.

As a result of the vision of the Royal Irish Academy which, from its foundation in 1785 made the collecting of archaeological objects from Ireland high on its list of priorities, and since its transfer in 1890 to the National Museum of Ireland, the collection has continued to grow either through new discoveries or the acquisition of private collections; today it is acknowedged as one of the largest and most important collections of Bronze Age gold in Western Europe.

Una de Blacam
Designer of Gold and Precious-Stone Jewelry

Una de Blacam lives with her husband, Shane, and thirteen-year-old daughter, Catherine, in a large mid-nineteenth-century house on Raglan Road, Dublin. The Georgian-style houses, with their mellow, rose-colored brick and fanlight doors, were designed to please rather than overawe.

Three roads, Waterloo, Wellington, and Raglan, lie parallel to each other; considering their close proximity to the city it is something of a miracle that the property developers have passed them by. They have remained virtually unchanged for well over a century and so exude an atmosphere of timelessness and permanency, perhaps because so many generations have gone before, often in the same house.

A parade of flowering cherry trees, mostly the coppery-leaved variety, *Prunus sargentii,* line the pavements. Some years, as early as the beginning of April, a combination of sun and rain (Shakespeare's "the uncertain glory of an April day") results in many trees being hazy with the first bronze leaves. A slight rise in temperature is all that is needed to tempt the pink blossom of the cherries to burst into flower like eager players waiting in the wings.

On such a day I visited Una de Blacam to talk to her about her gold jewelry.

Inside the de Blacam house everything is in subdued and exquisite taste; hardly surprising when one considers that Una's husband, Shane, is a distinguished architect whose firm, de Blacam and Meagher, has won many international awards for its work. Shafts of spring sunshine illuminate the spacious high-ceilinged rooms on the ground floor; we resist the temptation to linger in its balmy warmth, and instead resolutely make our way to the small room in the return of the first flight of stairs, which is Una's studio and workshop.

I ask her how she came to design and make jewelry, and what led her to the decision to work with gold.

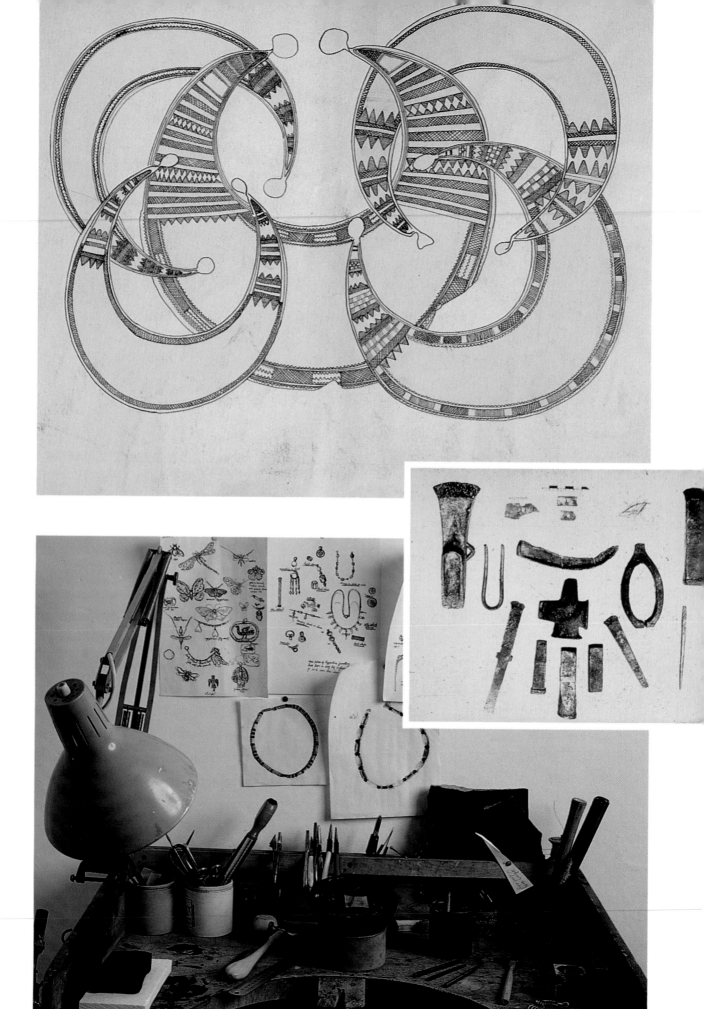

Una de Blacam at work on her gold and precious-stone jewelry.

I graduated from the National College of Art in Dublin, and then won a scholarship to the College of Art and Design in Oslo. Although as a student my area of specialization was painting, in Norway I worked mostly in the jewelry department.

After my return to Ireland, I began to design and make jewelry, mainly to commission. Following my marriage to Shane, we spent three years in Philadelphia. The Philadelphia Museum of Art, the University of Pennsylvania Museum, and the Rosenbach Museum were all sources of inspiration to me, as was the commercial jewelry district of that city. Other influences came from time spent in London, Oslo, and Perugia. But the first and most lasting influence has been that of Bronze Age Irish gold.

Una points to a drawing on the wall of her workshop executed during her student days. It is of five lunulae, one of the earliest and best known of the gold objects made in Ireland during the Bronze Age.

Even before I made the decision to design and make jewelry, I was strongly attracted to the simple shapes and geometric decorations of early Irish gold pieces. Later, I became interested in the techniques used to work the gold, chasing and repoussé, but the main attraction was the gold itself, so lavishly and freely used. Eventually jewelry became my chosen medium.

Una's necklaces are made from 18- or 22-karat gold. The technique used on most of the gold is what is known as repoussé work, that is, working on metal sheets with steel punches on a yielding surface, in this case, pitch. The strung gold bead necklaces and chains are the result of hour upon hour spent sitting at her workbench, bend-

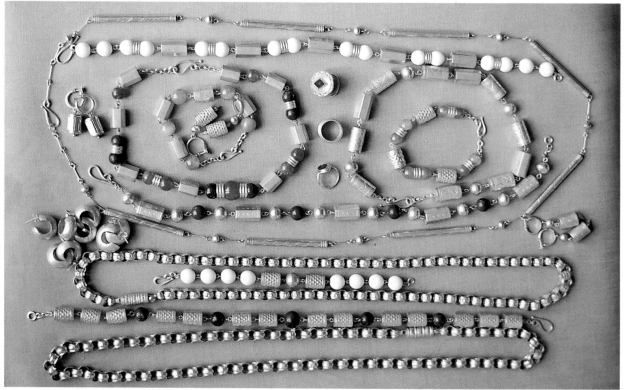

Beads of gold and precious stones from Una de Blacam's collection.

ing, tapping, beating—she points to the fact that the tools she uses to create her jewelry are remarkably similar to those used five thousand years ago by Bronze Age metal-workers. As with all crafts there are words relating to the tools and their uses which are foreign to the layman, a secret language understood only by those initiated in the ways of that particular craft.

Often the gold beads are used with gemstones. Una shows me her collection of stones which include coral, lapis lazuli, the latter polished and unpolished, moonstone pearls in the form of baroque beads, emeralds, and antique beads, some of them two thousand years old. I am attracted to a small rose-colored bead, in size no bigger than the nail on the little finger of my hand; I ask Una about the white marks which form a pattern on the bead. With the aid of a magnifying glass, she points out that the design is actually inlaid in the stone. One can only marvel at the skill of the craftsman who, thousands of years ago, created a distinct pattern to a high standard of excellence on such a small area.

There are some rings, which for the most part are settings for antique carved stones, usually Roman intaglios.

Looking around Una's workplace, I am amazed at its neatness. Pliers, hammers, and countless other tools whose names and uses are unknown to me are all within her reach, but stacked in an orderly fashion.

There is a certain almost hypnotic fascination in watching a craftsperson working in her chosen medium. The concentration and skill involved is remarkable and can only arouse in the beholder a high level of admiration for those individuals who, in this computer-dominated world, are dedicated to keeping alive the skills of our forefathers.

Emerging into the spring sunshine, my departure coincides with the entrance of the family pet, Pushkin, a handsome, long-haired black-and-white cat. In the supercilious manner of her breed, she looked me up but didn't bother to look me down.

Gown made from fabric of woven silver and gold threads.

Gold and Silver Threads

In many Asian countries where the early traditions of the use of fabric wholly or partly woven, ornamented, and embroidered with gold and silver have been maintained, the demand for such brilliant and costly textiles is still prevalent. In both the *Iliad* and the *Odyssey*, allusion is frequently made to woven and embroidered golden fabrics. The Persians in particular were celebrated as weavers and users of rich materials. Alexander the Great is said to have found eastern kings and princes "arrayed in robes of purple and gold."

From indications such as these, as well as those of a later date, one can see that the art of weaving and embroidery with gold and silver thread passed from one great city to another, traveling as a rule westward; Babylon, Baghdad, Damascus, the islands of Sicily and Cyprus, Venice, and southern Spain appear successively in the progress of time as centers of these most prized manufactures.

During the Middle Ages, European royal personages and high ecclesiastical dignitaries used cloth and tissue of gold and silver for their state and ceremonial robes, as well as for costly hangings and decoration.

The thin flimsy paper known as tissue paper is so called because it originally was placed between folds of gold tissue (or weaving) to prevent the contiguous surfaces from fraying each other.

The association of gold with kingship is very ancient. In the early part of this century, a firm in northern Ireland received a commission from a royal household to design and weave a fabric using unbleached Irish linen yarn and pure gold thread. The result is a material of exquisite design and quality, possibly unique in its combination of natural fibers.

Fabric woven of unbleached Irish linen yarn and pure gold thread.

Silver

Silver is an element known from the earliest times, and of great importance as a metal for articles of value — coinage, ornamentation, and jewelry. The word "silver" probably refers to the shining appearance and brightness of the metal. The alchemists named it Luna or Diana and denoted it by the crescent moon; the first name has survived in lunar caustic, silver nitrate. In appearance silver presents a pure white color with a perfect metallic luster. It is the most malleable and pliant of all metals, with the exception of gold. One gram can be drawn out into a wire 590 feet

Double sauceboat of Irish silver.

long, and the leaf can be beaten out to a thickness of 0.00025mm, but traces of arsenic, antimony, bismuth, or lead make it brittle. In hardness it is superior to gold, but inferior to copper. Silver in an absolutely pure form is too soft for practical use, so it is mixed with another metal, an alloy, in most instances copper, to provide the necessary hardness. Sterling silver is metal of not less than 92.5 percent pure silver; the remaining 7.5 percent of the alloy is not prescribed, but is usually copper.

Objects of gold have been made in Ireland for at least four thousand years. The introduction of Christianity about A.D. 500 led to a period when both silver and gold were worked on with a skill rivaling, and even exceeding, the rest of Europe. This period, which lasted in varying degrees up to 1500, produced such world-famous objects as the Ardagh Chalice, the Cross of Cong, and the Derrynaflan hoard, the latter found in Tipperary in 1980. Such pieces reflected an amazing technical virtuosity and an artistry which mirrored the increasing sophistication of the craftsmen.

The influence of Christianity was very strong. The Church was the channel through which flowed inspiration from the Mediterranean countries and western Europe.

In the late sixth century, many pilgrim monks began to leave Ireland to spread Christianity in Britain, Germany, France, and Italy. They founded monasteries in those countries, and manuscripts preserved in European libraries ensure that the memory of their achievements is kept alive. In return, the Irish craftsman, whatever his medium, was refreshed by this contact, and it meant an exchange of cultures, all of which was reflected in the arts and crafts of those times.

Probably because of its proximity, the culture and art of Ireland and Britain were closely interwoven with one another during the early Christian era. A series of brooches, dating from A.D. 700, being crafted in Scotland as well as England, led to the development of Ireland's famous Tara Brooch.

It was perhaps inevitable that the monasteries and their obvious signs of prosperity should attract the attention of the Vikings toward the end of the eighth century. The invaders interrupted but did not abolish the making of fine metal, but the fact that fragments of beautiful Irish-made objects are often found in Viking graves in Norway tell their own story. On the other hand, the invaders brought increasing supplies of raw material probably from Koonsberg in Norway, where massive supplies of silver were available.

Commissions for important objects continued throughout the Viking age—the Derrynaflan Chalice is one of them. The outstanding beauty of this piece bears witness to an extraordinary artistry—it has eighty-four filigree panels and fifty-seven amber studs. Of all the hard gemstones, it was amber that was used most frequently by Irish craftsmen.

The native tradition survived the Vikings and flourished once again in the eleventh and twelfth centuries.

Chalices form the vast bulk of the pieces made from silver which have survived from 1500 to 1660, but after that, articles intended for domestic use predominate.

In 1637 Charles I granted a charter which established the Company of Goldsmiths of Dublin, a term that also applies to silversmiths, and gave it extensive powers to control the manufacture and sale of gold and silver in Ireland. In April 1638 the first piece of silver was assayed and hallmarked. The charter prescribed two marks for silver—the goldsmith's proper mark, which was the maker's mark, and the harp crowned, which certified the correct fineness. The company itself introduced the date letter, a letter of the alphabet representing the year of assay. These have remained virtually unchanged since 1890.

Each silversmith would have registered his mark with the masters and wardens of the Goldsmith Company. The article was submitted for testing and if the silver content was found to be less than 92.5 percent, the article was smashed and returned to

*Tea table set with three-legged silver sugar bowl and Irish silver
potato ring. Potato rings were popular in the eighteenth century.
A bowl of potatoes was set inside the rim to preserve the
surface of the dining table.*

the owner. If it contained the correct percentage of silver, it was stamped with a hallmark. Standards were inflexible, and even the loveliest items were destroyed if they did not contain the right amount of silver. There were heavy fines for breaking the rules. The same standards apply today.

The term "Irish Silver" popularly refers to fine objects made in Ireland from the seventeenth through the nineteenth centuries. Nature has always been a source of inspiration for artists—acanthus leaves, flowers, and fruit, often in the company of animals and birds, which appeared as decoration on a variety of pieces.

Between the years 1700 and 1740 plain silver was the most popular, with attention concentrated on shape and proportion rather than on decoration. Circular, square, hexagonal, and octagonal pieces were made and the decoration was simply a cartouche which might confine a coat of arms.

Around 1735 the straitjacket symmetry gave way to a style to which the eminent architect of his time, Sir William Temple, gave the name "Sharawadji," a particular word to express a studied irregularity. Probably the word derives either from the Chinese *sa-ro (k) wai chi,* meaning "graceful disorder" or the Japanese *soro-wa-ji,* "not being symmetrical."

By 1750 Dublin had become the second largest city in the British Empire, and was noted for its high level of culture. Undoubtedly the Irish silversmith was influenced by the graceful Georgian city with its handsome squares and town houses. The city's appearance was in no small measure due to the influence of the architect, James Gandon (1743–1824). Many of Dublin's public buildings with their imposing classical details were designed by Gandon. Certainly many of the pieces of silver crafted during that period reflect the elegance of the city at that time.

The late Georgian and Regency period saw considerable economic growth which created an atmosphere that allowed Irish architecture and the decorative arts, including silver, to flourish. The various styles of Irish silver crafted during the period from 1660 to the beginning of the nineteenth century reflect influences from Britain and other European countries. There are, however, types of articles and decorative features considered to be intrinsically Irish—the three-legged bowl is one, but perhaps the best-known example is the dish ring. This was a stand designed to support a bowl containing hot food to keep the heat from marring the surface of the table.

After 1770 the newly excavated sites of Pompeii and Herculaneum influenced designers across Europe, including Ireland. The styles began to be inspired by Greek and Roman art; the shapes changed and became more classical, and decorations included laurel leaves and medallions.

By the middle of the nineteenth century there had been a renewed interest in the early history of Ireland. This, together with the discovery of ancient objects almost uniquely Celtic in character—the Tara Brooch found near the mouth of the river Boyne in 1850 and the Ardagh Chalice in 1868 in County Limerick—led the way to a neo-Celtic style which to a lesser degree exists to the present day.

Donald MacPherson
Master Silversmith

onald MacPherson is a master craftsman of handmade precious metals.
He was a latecomer to this ancient craft,
having qualified as a master silversmith at
the age of fifty-five.

I first met this remarkable man through
John Teahan, Keeper of the Art and Industrial Division of the National Museum of
Ireland. John's friendship with Donald
came about through an initial rejection of a
silver miniature of a Georgian door, measuring ten inches high, made at Donald's
Calderwood School of Silversmithing. Despite the rejection John Teahan was impressed by the quality of the
workmanship in the piece. He
met some of the silversmiths
whom Donald had trained and
inspected their work—silver
made as it was during the seventeenth and eighteenth centuries—and this inspired him
with the idea that the craft,
with all its ancient techniques,
should be represented in the
museum as part of a special exhibition being mounted to cele-

brate Ireland's Year of Culture (1991).

Since that time Donald, and the pupils
from his silver school, have a permanent
exhibition of their work—pieces include
goblets, beakers, bowls, chalices, ewers, and
small silver caskets—at the museum.

An invitation to visit him at his home
was accepted with alacrity. It took little
prompting from me to encourage him to
tell his story, and an interesting one it was.

Born in Dublin in 1914, one of a family
of six children, he left Ireland in 1932, ambitious to "conquer the world." Arriving in
England with no money, he applied for
whatever agricultural and
laboring jobs were available.
In 1933 he obtained a steady
position as a groom on the
Cheshire estate of Lieutenant-
Colonel Moncrief-Carr.
Grooming the horses only
took a few hours of the working day, so he also acted as a
valet to the colonel, and as a
footman in the dining room;
it was in this latter capacity
that he was responsible for

the condition of the household silver. It was his first close contact with silver and he fell in love with what he describes as "the queen of metals."

In 1936 because of time-absorbing business pressures, the colonel gave up horse riding, so was no longer in need of the services of a groom. As a mark of appreciation for Donald's service to the family, the colonel recommended him to a job in the Stretford and District Gas Board, where he stayed until the outbreak of war in 1939.

On his arrival in England in 1932, Donald had joined the Territorial Army, but, in truth, it was mainly to enjoy the benefit of the boots, overcoat, and kit that they handed out to new recruits. However, in 1939 with the outbreak of hostilities, he was summoned to report for duty.

That he had an aptitude for mechanical things soon became obvious; he was put in charge of an antiaircraft unit equipped with Bofurs guns. As the war progressed, he trained as a gunnery instructor, and was promoted to corporal and then sergeant.

In August 1944 his unit crossed over to Normandy, from there they embarked on a Swedish ship which crossed the North Sea, eventually making its way up the Oslo Fjord, where they disembarked. A framed certificate of merit signed by Prince (now King) Olav of Norway, which hangs on the wall of the workshop in his home, testifies to his contribution to the cessation of hostilities in Norway.

When the war ended Donald went back to his job of pipe laying in the gas company. One day on a site in Leicestershire he made a tiny boiler for the toy steam engine belonging to the son of one of the engineers. The boy's father was impressed with Donald's work, and remarked that it was a pity that he, Donald, had not become a coppersmith. But silver was Donald's love and having quietly reflected on what the engineer had said he decided, at the age of fifty-three, to enter the nearby Luftborough College to study to be a silversmith. Later he studied a further two years at Liverpool College of Art, becoming a master silversmith at the age of fifty-five. At the end of the course, the principal of the college announced that Donald was the only potential silversmith in the class.

Another of his hobbies was traveling: he journeyed across China and Mongolia and traversed the Soviet Union aboard the Trans-Siberian Express. However, in 1974 he decided that his traveling days were over and he returned to Ireland to indulge himself in his newfound love of silversmithing.

He bought a house in Marino, north Dublin, within a mile of the sea, just yards away from the home he had left almost fifty years earlier. Donald explains:

My dream was to start a school to preserve the craft of the Irish silversmith. It is a craft which had been indigenous to Ireland for well over a thousand years, and some of the greatest silver work in the world was done in this country. I set about converting one of the rooms in my house into a workplace for my own use; then in 1984 I was fortunate in finding a room at the back of a boys' school in north Dublin within walking distance of my home; this became the Donald MacPherson, Calderwood School of Silversmithing, Calderwood after the great eighteenth-century silversmith of that name.

To the eye of a layman, the workshop of a silversmith appears to be chaotic. There are anvils

Tools in Donald MacPherson's workshop.

which are also called raising stakes on which the disks of silver are placed for hammering into the required shape. The all-important hammer comes in a variety of sizes, there are special tools for chasing and piercing, a metal stake called a horse, a buffalo horn mallet—it goes on and on.

In the small workshop the students gather and shape silver disks into beakers, chalices, goblets, and so on. All the work is done as far as possible as it was in the seventeenth and eighteenth centuries; obviously there are some changes such as using gas for the smelting and welding. In fact, my only concession to modern technology is using portable propane gas, and it is with some regret that I have to resort to such a device, but the hammering, the tens of thousands of taps which shape the metal, it is the same craft as of old.

Nothing is wasted, engineering lathes are carefully stored, tools are liable to be fashioned from an old trailer tow bar, or from part of a pipe that I used in England when I worked for the gas company. It seems that at one time or another every tool in the workshop has led another life.

Irish Hands

Donald MacPherson fashioning a silver christening

I ask Donald to describe the processes to me, and where possible to demonstrate them. As he explained it, the method is as follows:

A disk of silver cut to size is placed over the anvil and hammered. The silversmith works round and round the disk, gradually moving toward the center, by which time the flat disk has been raised to the shape of a saucer. The hammering will have changed the atomic structure of the metal so it becomes hard and brittle, and it will have to be put through a process where it is subjected to intense heat and then allowed to cool slowly—this process is called annealing, and it restores the pliability of the metal.

The disk is then placed over a small anvil, known as a raising stake, another hammering

session takes place, this time from the center out-ward, the hammering continues until the silver-smith is satisfied that the required shape is formed—sometimes to achieve this the craftsman might have to hammer the disk as many as two hundred times. By now the piece is covered with obtrusive hammer marks. To remove them a technique known as planishing is applied; the body of the piece is hammered with a flat ham-mer covered with a heavy leather cap. This leaves small irregular marks on the surface of the article, which give handmade silver its character.

At this moment there are nine budding silver-smiths in the school. I believe that four are nat-urals and will go on to great things. My waiting list of students ranges from foreign diplomats to clerical workers.

Donald's work and that of his pupils are entered in appropriate competitions. They have won many prestigious awards. Donald was overall winner of the Ford/Evening Herald Cultural Award, the citation for which paid tribute to his vision, determina-tion, independence, and talent. The objects he is most proud of making are a silver beaker, a gold goblet, and a platinum beaker; he calls them his Three Graces.

During my army career I drank out of a variety of vessels—jam jars, tin cans, even steel helmets. I promised myself that if I survived the war I would make, for my own use, drinking vessels fit for a king—and I did, and what is more I use them every weekend—the silver beaker is in use on Friday, the gold goblet on Saturday, and the platinum beaker is drunk out of on Sunday.

Donald's remaining ambition is to have more space to take some of his country-wide students off the waiting list. "I want to leave the craft in safe hands, to see it carried on—it must not be allowed to die." Of special pleasure to him is the fact that people, including our esteemed President, Mary Robinson, are supporting craftspeople with specially commissioned pieces. This, Donald believes, is the way forward for the retention of many ancient crafts.

The Irish Table

Cheesemaking
Honey and Beekeeping

Cheesemaking

According to mythology the invention of cheese was ascribed to Artistaeus, the son of Apollo by the nymph, Cyrene. The derivation of the word comes from the Latin caseus, and, in German, Dutch, Irish, Welsh, and English before A.D. 1100 it was käse, kaas, cais, caws, and cyse respectively. Later in England, it became coese or cease,

and in the sixteenth and seventeenth centuries ches, chies, and schese. Cheese is a solidified preparation from milk, the essential component of which is the proteinous or nitrogenous substance, casein. In addition all cheese contains some proportion of fatty matter or butter and in the more expensive varieties the butter present is often greater in amount than the casein. So cheese is a

compound substance of no definite composition and is found in many different varieties and qualities, and such qualities are generally recognized by the name of the localities in which they are made. The principal distinctions arise from differences in the composition and condition of the milk used, from variations in the method of preparation and curing, and from the use of milk from animals other than cows, for example, goats and sheep, from whose milk cheese is made on a commercial scale. Like wine, cheese probably came into being by sheer accident. Persia or Turkey may well have seen its birth when some wandering traveler placed his daily supply of goat's milk in a bag made from animal skin or intestines, hoisted himself on his beast of burden, and went on his way. The animal's movement and the hot sun separated the curd from the whey, which could account for ordinary cheese.

Various references to cheese are to be found in early Irish literature indicating its general use as a food from the early Christian period. However, only in a few instances is any descriptive information given other than the name of the cheese. An example of names and descriptions applied to certain cheeses is given in the twelfth-century poem, *The Vision of Mac Conglinne,* which has been described as a unique social picture of twelfth-century Ireland. A number of references to names and descriptions of different cheeses are made in the text: tanach, described as firm and comparatively dry, and maothal, which is referred to as a soft, sweet, smooth cheese.

From prehistoric times up to the end of the seventeenth century the food Irish people ate was wholesome and in great variety. Rivers and sea yielded large harvests of fish: salmon was a particular favorite. The markets of medieval Dublin offered strawberries, raspberries, damsons, sloes, cherries, and blackberries from the Dublin hills; pears, plums, and apples are often mentioned in early sagas, luxuries like almonds, figs, raisins, and walnuts were imported by the spice ships of southern Europe. Corn and milk were the mainstay of the population.

Almost every farmhouse had a dairy with rows of gleaming pans and strainers where the dairymaid or the woman of the house made cheese. Traditional cheeses included tanach, a hard pressed skim-milk cheese, which indications from early literature suggest was pressed in small molds; gruth, a curdy cheese made from buttermilk or skim milk; mulchan, made of buttermilk beaten to form a soft cheese which was then pressed and molded; and milsfan, which appears to have been a sweet curd cheese or junket made from sweet milk. Cream cheese was popular and made with thick rich cream, a pinch of salt, and a little dry mustard, all of which were placed in a jelly bag or straining cloth, usually hung between two chairs with a basin underneath to catch the drops. When the cheese solidified, which took about twenty-four hours in a cool dairy, it was turned into a mold and pressed under a butterweight until firm.

Most cheese was made from cow's milk, though goat's milk cheese was eaten and considered very nourishing.

Throughout the whole of the long period, from pre-Christian Ireland to the middle of the eighteenth century, cheese was a staple food.

During the eighteenth century, the making and consumption of cheese in Ireland progressively declined. By the early nineteenth century the decline in cheesemaking had gone so far that agricultural writers of

the time stated that little or none was made. This state of affairs was partly due to the unsettled conditions prevailing during the sixteenth and seventeenth centuries arising from the various wars and land confiscations. There were also other factors which contributed to the direction taken by agricultural production in Ireland. It became more economical for the milk to be turned into butter. By 1800 Ireland was the most important exporter of butter in the world. As the butter industry grew, the economic condition of the farmers improved, but the craft of cheesemaking declined, and a food for which the Irish were justly famous was seldom eaten.

Cheesemaking cropped up from time to time during this two hundred-year period, sometimes in individual houses for private use, but also for a limited market such as in County Kilkenny, where in 1800 sheep's milk cheese was produced. In the 1940s some French nuns, members of the Franciscan Mission of Mary, at Loughlyn in County Roscommon, made an excellent Pont l'Eveque. Then, in the 1970s, Veronica Steele, who might be described as the earth mother of the farmhouse cheese industry in Ireland, inherited a small farm overlooking Kenmare Bay on the Beara Peninsula in southwest Cork, and started to make cheese. One of the cheeses, the now-famous Milleens, was made to one of those central European recipes accredited to the ancient Irish monks, who would have left Ireland voluntarily, as missionaries in the late sixth century or fled the country during the Viking invasion of the eighth century, when the wealth of the monasteries as a source of provisions and other goods attracted the attention of the Viking ma-rauders. Undoubtedly cheesemaking would have been one of the talents the monks took with them and practiced in their new homes.

The making of Milleens was a turning point when cheesemaking started to come into fashion again, probably as it was origi-nally made, with many different consisten-cies and flavors. Veronica Steele had released a landslide into farmhouse cheese-making. It is significant that her enterprise coincided with the coming of milk quotas. Perhaps for the first time since 1650, it paid to be in cheesemaking.

Veronica's neighbors became interested in her success, and she began to share her knowledge with them. The pioneers were generous with their knowledge and experi-ence and the numbers of producers grew substantially. Today there are around forty-five farmhouse cheese producers making tons of cheese each year, some 50 percent of which is consumed in the home market. Many of the Irish cheeses have found im-portant export markets in Britain, France and Belgium, Germany, Canada, and the United States, which could be a reflection of the fact that the consumer demand is in-creasing for individual products of quality, rather than the monotony of mass produc-tion.

Farmhouse cheeses are one of the success stories of Irish agriculture. When they first appeared about twelve years ago, they seemed to be going right against the trend of agricultural development. They were produced by small-scale operators, using traditional methods and making a product for a limited and not wholly defined mar-ket. But they established themselves rapidly and showed the way for a very important side of Irish farming. Above all, they proved the point that the future lay in quality and not quantity.

Veronica Steele

Milleens Farmhouse Cheesemaker

Veronica Steele, acknowledged as being the standard-bearer for the farmhouse cheesemakers, lives with her husband Norman and their children on a farm in a far-flung corner of southwest Ireland, a place of great natural beauty.

In her own inimitable way she tells how she came to make Milleens, the cheese which led to the birth of the farmhouse cheese industry, and how she graduated from cutting her teeth on cheddar to Champion Cheesemaker of Milleens, and in doing so opened the door to a whole new agricultural dimension.

Achieving a modicum of fame as a cheesemaker never figured in my dreams when I was growing up. I fantasized about becoming an actress, singer, writer, and even an acrobat, but never in my wildest fantasy did I dream of becoming a celebrated cheesemaker. "Well respected within the trade" is actually a fine accolade.

In 1968, aged twenty, I graduated in logic and philosophy. A few months later I was introduced to

Norman, also a philosophy graduate, and with little ado we began philosophizing together in a romantic whitewashed cottage in the parish of Allihies, on the Beara Peninsula in County Cork. The following autumn Norman became a lecturer at Trinity College, Dublin. For the next eight years he commuted between County Cork and Dublin, until the magnetic magic of Beara became irresistible and he resigned his post at Trinity.

During these years the first two of our four children had been born, and we had bought Milleens, a farm in Eyeries, the neighboring parish to Allihies. We also bought a cow. Her name was Brisket, and she only had one horn which gave her appearance a comical one-sided look. She gave us three gallons of milk a day and I didn't quite know what to do with it all.

I began to make cheddar cheese, but without a great deal of success. One day Norman said, "Why don't you try making a soft cheese for a change?" So I did. At first it failed and failed again, but each failed effort

*A picnic with Veronica Steele's Milleens
cheese and Irish whole-meal bread.*

spurred me on to a greater understanding of the process, until eventually the door to microbiology opened for me.

While all this was going on, Norman was planting a large vegetable garden full of fresh spinach, zucchini, French beans, and little peas, all the vegetables one could not buy in the local shops. The surplus he sold to a friend, Annie Goulding, who was chef at The Blue Bull restaurant in Sneem, a neighboring town.

Annie's reputation as a first-class cook was known throughout Ireland and beyond. She maintained that one of the secrets of her success was the lengths she was prepared to go to in order to ensure that the ingredients used were the best available. Annie would go down to the harbor to await the arrival of the fishing boats, and then badger the fishermen for the pick of their catch. Early every Monday morning she would come to our farm to wander in the vegetable garden looking for the freshest and best of the crop.

Each Monday in preparation for her visit, I would have ready for her to take away batches of yogurt, pies made with hare and cream, pork pies and fish pies all decked about with pastry leaves and rosettes, and my specialty, profiteroles oozing chocolate and cream. And then one day, about fifteen years ago, we wrapped up some of my runny soft cheese and away it went with the other good things to make its debut at The Blue Bull.

By an almost miraculous coincidence, Declan Ryan of the Arbutus Lodge Hotel in Cork and Myrtle Allen of Ballymaloe House, two of Ireland's greatest luminaries of culinary art, were dining, in separate parties, at The Blue Bull that night. They each concluded their meals with slivers of the first Milleens cheese. Both were excited and impressed with its flavor and texture.

We still supply Milleens to our first customers, Annie Goulding, Declan Ryan, and Myrtle Allen. Anyone will try a product once out of simple curiosity; to keep buying it for the next ten years tells you something about that product.

For the past ten years we have devoted our energies to the continued improvement and development of our cheese; it is an ongoing occupation. Vast quantities of learning have been ingested and applied, from the many journals on dairy science through scientific pamphlets on bacteriology.

The making of Milleens is not a slaphappy matter, but a carefully controlled scientific process. Thermometers have replaced elbows; pH and acidity is noted, milk quality is carefully monitored. Starters are recognized as a most important influence on flavor and quality and are as well looked after as the crown jewels. Milleens is no longer seasonal.

Milleens has had a profound influence on the consumption of dairy products on the home market and on the development of new ones. We have stimulated and encouraged more cheesemakers through teaching, giving advice and, in close cooperation with the National Dairy Council, the founding of Cais, the Association of Irish Farmhouse Cheesemakers.

In 1990 we received the Food and Wine from France trophy for the best soft cheese at the London International Show, beating the competition from Germany, Britain, and even France.

We have established a firm home base for Milleens which expands steadily and strongly; no sooner is one phase of growth completed before another begins. Milleens is no longer alone, but forms the nucleus of a generation of cheeses which have developed in its wake. Some ten years ago on my first meeting with Declan Ryan, we talked of the future and I confided to him an ambition that in twenty years Ireland would have a regional cheese industry to be proud of.

Local cheeses would help to stimulate a vast prosperous parallel factory industry. This has happened and a dream has been realized.

Paddy and Juliet Berridge
Carrigbyrne Farmhouse

arrigbyrne Farmhouse, home of the Berridge family, lies just a mile or so beyond the small village of Adamstown in County Wexford. This county shares with Tipperary the reputation of enjoying the best farmland in the whole of Ireland. Villages such as Adamstown nestle comfortably into the heart of the local countryside as they have done for centuries: small terraced houses have a uniformity which suggests that they were linked to a large house in the sort of paternal relationship which existed in many Irish villages a generation or so ago. On this late spring day we are on our way to visit Paddy and Juliet Berridge to talk to them about their famous Saint Killian Camembert-type cheese, and their comparatively new Saint Brendan Brie.

Although the city is barely thirty miles behind us, already one begins to feel the healing power of the countryside: whereas

city life is full of inward thoughts and urgent destinations, no hint of turbulence is allowed to disrupt these inviolate fields. The latter part of our journey finds us on a narrow, meandering country road, on either side of which are thick carpets of Queen Anne's lace. Trees are puffed out in clouds of light green foliage, meadows are golden with buttercups, and ferns uncurl at the base of the hedgerows.

Upon arrival at Carrigbyrne we are greeted by Paddy and Juliet and two of their three children, Jenny and Charlie (Richard, the eldest, is away at boarding school). While David is choosing his sites for photography, Paddy and I sit apart from the others, so that we can talk about how he came to make his now-famous cheeses.

The beginning was actually a long time ago, because he admits that from the tender age of

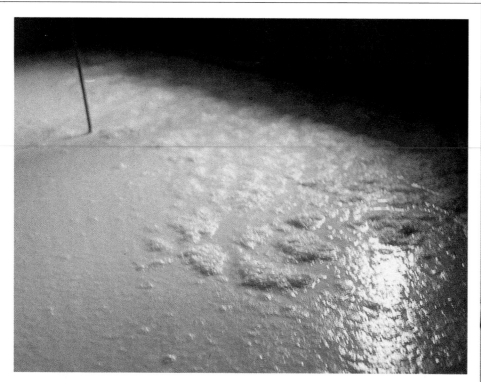

Hexagonal metal containers filled with Paddy Berridge's Saint Killian, a Camembert-type cheese.

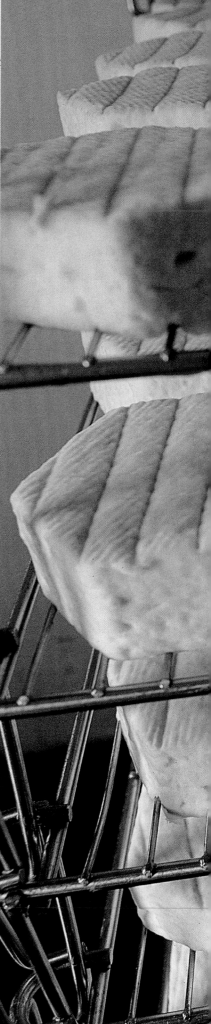

Irish Hands

seven years he showed an interest in the culinary arts. He claims this interest is due to the fact that his mother is Belgian. His formal education behind him, Paddy returned to the family farm and married Juliet Roche from a neighboring estate.

He soon realized that the farm on its own was not a viable proposition. Farmhouse cheese, handmade by traditional methods, was just beginning to find a market in Ireland after centuries of neglect. Having made up his mind that this was the course he wished to pursue, he went to France and learned his cheesemaking skills in a French Camembert factory in Normandy. Upon his return to Ireland he set about converting the farm outbuildings which surround the nineteenth-century cobblestone courtyard behind the family house into a dairy for making handmade cheese, installing the most up-to-date equipment available.

Realizing that this comparatively new facet of Irish agriculture would need careful and imaginative marketing, Paddy decided to employ a production manager with experience in cheesemaking in order to allow him the freedom to study the market. That was ten years ago; now Alain Girode from France regards Ireland as his second home, and has since been joined by three local men.

Paddy continues:

With so much competition on the market I sought ways of making Carrigbyrne cheese easily identifiable, and came up with the distinctive hexagonal shape of our Camembert-type cheese, Saint Killian. The latter has now been joined by Saint Brendan Brie, a well-matured full-fat
cow's milk cheese, which we make in two sizes, a small one-kilo Brie and the higher fat large wheel Brie. It is a 100 percent natural product, with no added flavoring or coloring. Salt is the only preservative used.

Both cheeses are made from Irish milk provided by our own Carrigbyrne herd of Fresian cows. The milk is pumped to the most up-to-date cheesemaking equipment, housed in the original stone farm outbuildings.

The essential quality of a farmhouse cheese is that it is an individual product. It is made from the milk of one herd which gives it a special character and identity. It is always a natural product to the extent that any one cheese is never the same from one batch to another.

Extensive quality control testing by an independent laboratory is carried out from the raw milk stage through to the matured, finished cheeses; this ensures a top-quality product of which we are extremely proud.

I suggest that for a country of such rich dairy land the apparent lack of a cheesemaking tradition is strange. Paddy replies:

Actually, cheesemaking in Ireland goes back a long time and was only interrupted by the general turmoil of the late nineteenth century. Cheese continued to be made in many parts of the country well into the last century, but it was mainly for household consumption on the farms and country estates on which it was made. Butter was the cash product which took most of the milk.

It is time for us to visit the dairy. Stepping from the charming nineteenth-century courtyard into the clinical atmosphere of the dairy is to move from one world into an-

Brie-type Saint Brendan cheese and Camembert-type
Saint Killian in wicker baskets with fruit.

other. Alain Girode and his team are dressed from head to toe in what can only be described as sparkling white. Great vats of milk are aided at different stages of their journey into cheese by marvelous futuristic-looking steel appliances. The floor is constantly being hosed with water, and Wellington boots would be a more suitable footwear, I decide, as I hop from one foot to the other in a futile effort to keep my feet dry. This is a world far removed from that of the jellybag hanging between two chairs, with a basin underneath to catch the drops, as cheesemaking would have been done half a century ago.

We have an opportunity to taste the

Saint Brendan Brie, deep-fried and served with hot toast and red currant jelly, as a first course of a delicious luncheon prepared by Juliet. After lunch we move into the drawing room for coffee and a tasting of a rare liqueur.

This is a beautiful room, large with exceptionally high ceilings. Juliet tells us that in the early part of this century it was often the scene of the local Hunt Ball. It is easy to imagine these walls echoing to the sound of music mingling with high-pitched voices and jolly laughter.

I am drawn toward the huge bay window at one end of the room. It looks over acres of Berridge land. A single large tree is providing shelter for what appears to be the entire Carrigbyrne herd. How peaceful it all is: this is a landscape of consolation as reassuring as the most placid views Constable produced near his own home in the Stour Valley.

Honey and Beekeeping

Beekeeping, or the cultivation of the honeybee as a source of income to those who practice it, is known to have existed from earliest times. It is probable that humans have

been harvesting honey for at least ten thousand years. Some five thousand years ago, in the dimness of prehistory, the Sumerians founded modern civilization in a region where the rivers Tigris and Euphrates flow south to the Persian Gulf—the land between the rivers was called Mesopotamia and it was there that the gradual change from the nomadic life to agriculture took place.

The love poetry of the Sumerians shows that honey was no stranger to this earliest of civilizations: "more fragrant than honey" are the caresses of the bride. It is possible that the hanging gardens of Babylon were inhabited by bees, although they would have been wild specimens for it was to be another few thousand years before it occurred to man to house bees in some sort of hive. The most graphic accounts of beekeeping in ancient times come from Egyptian tombs, where the first recorded hives can be seen. On the sarcophagus containing the mummified body of Mykerinos, dating back to twenty-sixth century B.C., can be found a hieroglyphic bee representing the King of Lower Egypt; it serves as an illustration of the manner in which the bee was recognized as the embodiment of government by a chief or ruler in

Father Kelly checking a skep. These earliest known beehives
are made of straw and blackberry twigs.

ancient times. The bee as royal motif was also adopted by Napoleon and, among other things, it embellished his royal cape.

The Old Testament is full of references to honey. The manna which sustained the Israelites in the wilderness is thought to have been honey. The Koran also acknowledges the importance of bees and the soothing powers of honey.

Such was the position of bees and their keepers in Greek society that they had their special patron god, Aristaeus. According to legend he was the son of Apollo and the nymph, Cyrene. The same Aristaeus is sometimes claimed as being the patron god of cheesemakers also. Galen, the first-century Greek physician, recommended honey for coughs and colds, bronchitis, and asthmatic conditions. Aristotle was a bee-keeper and honey was at the top of his list of healing substances. Pliny also recognized its value in the treatment of eye disorders (probably cataracts). Hippocrates, believed to be the father of all medicine, was particularly partial to honey; he recommended it as part of a simple diet, and also, in conjunction with vinegar, as a painkiller. Pliny and Virgil wrote extensively about bees and honey. In fact, poets, philosophers, historians, and naturalists through the ages have eulogized the bee as being unique among insects, endowed by nature with wondrous gifts beneficial to humans in a greater degree than any other of the insect world.

In Ireland hives were almost certainly used from pre-Christian times. Early hives were probably skeps (baskets) made of woven wicker and later of coiled straw.

The dome-shaped straw skep of our forefathers may be regarded as the typical bee-hive of all time and of all civilized countries; indeed, it may with truth be said that as a healthy and convenient home for the honeybee it still has no equal. A swarm of bees hived in a straw skep, the picturesque little domicile known the world over as the personification of industry, will furnish their homes with waxen combs in form and shape so admirably adapted to their requirements as to need no improvement by man. Much of our knowledge of medieval and earlier honey producing comes from *Bechbretha,* a part of the Ancient Laws of Ireland.

Opinions differ as to whether the honeybee was introduced to Britain and Ireland by man, or made its own way to these countries when there was still a land connection with the Continent. One belief is that a swarm of honeybees was brought from Britain by the saint Mo Domnoc, who lived in the early sixth century A.D.

According to legend the youthful Mo Domnoc set out for Wales to study at the feet of the great Saint David. He remained many years in the monastery, where his special care was beehives which formed part of the abbey's wealth. When at length the time came for Mo Domnac to return to Ireland his little friends refused to be parted from him. Three times they followed him to the ship waiting to set sail for Ireland, and three times he bore them back to their hives. In the end Saint David presented the swarm of bees to his friend and disciple. He blessed the bees with the words: "May the land to which you are brought abound with your progeny and may their species and generation never fail, but our own city shall forever be deprived of you, nor shall your seed any longer increase in it." The

prophecy was fulfilled, for the Welsh bees prospered and multiplied in their new home, their honey was ever sweet and the green forests of Ireland were perfumed by that sweetness, but no bees were afterward found in Saint David's monastery of Menevia, where David ruled.

Another charming legend refers to Saint Gobnait of Ballyvourney, County Cork, who is regarded as the patron saint of beekeepers. Her feast, like Saint Mo Domnoc's, occurs in the month of February, and like him, she is reputed to have lived sometime in the sixth century. The legend of her dealing with bees is told in many parts of Munster, and many variants of the story are contained in the manuscript material of the Department of Irish Folklore. The story goes that an invading chief and his army descended on the country around Ballyvourney, with plunder in mind. Their plan was to despoil the land and rob the cattle. She prayed for guidance and then let loose the bees. The bees stung the marauding chieftain and his followers so sharply that the cowardly men fled for their lives. Their work done, the bees dutifully returned to the hive and the making of honey.

Early saints were credited with the introduction of a number of agricultural and other techniques, some of which are known from archaeological evidence to be of far greater antiquity. The truth may be that monasteries practiced beekeeping on a larger scale than was known in pre-Christian Ireland, and so acquired the reputation of having introduced it.

The linguistic evidence suggests that Irish acquaintance with the honeybee is a lot older than the fifth and sixth centuries. The old Irish language has native words for bee, honey, and mead. The principal word for bee in Irish is *bech,* it is cognate with Old English *beo.* The Irish word for honey is *mil* which is cognate with the Welsh, Cornish, and Breton *mel* and Greek *meli. Mell* is the Latin for honey. Certain place names often incorporate the word honey. Mellifont Abbey, near Drogheda, was the home of the Cistercian monks in Ireland. The name is derived from two Latin words: *fons mellis* (the source of honey); Clonmel (Clun Mell), the meadow of honey, is another example.

This evidence indicates that the honeybee was present in Ireland long before the arrival of Christianity.

Monasteries all over Europe were important centers of honey production. Not only was honey the source of sweetness but beeswax candles provided pure clear light. To this day these candles are used on the high altar. Beeswax was also used on weapons and other metal surfaces to prevent rusting. The kitchen and medicine chest also benefited from the honey. It was still the only sweetening agent and played an important part in all the old established recipes such as gingerbread. It wasn't until the sixteenth century that sugar made from cane and beets became the universal cheap sweetener.

However, in those days there was considerable confusion about how honey actually was made. Gradually over the centuries there was a vague understanding that the quality of honey was related to the quality of the flowers; and in the nineteenth century the puzzle of how bees reproduced themselves was, at last, properly understood.

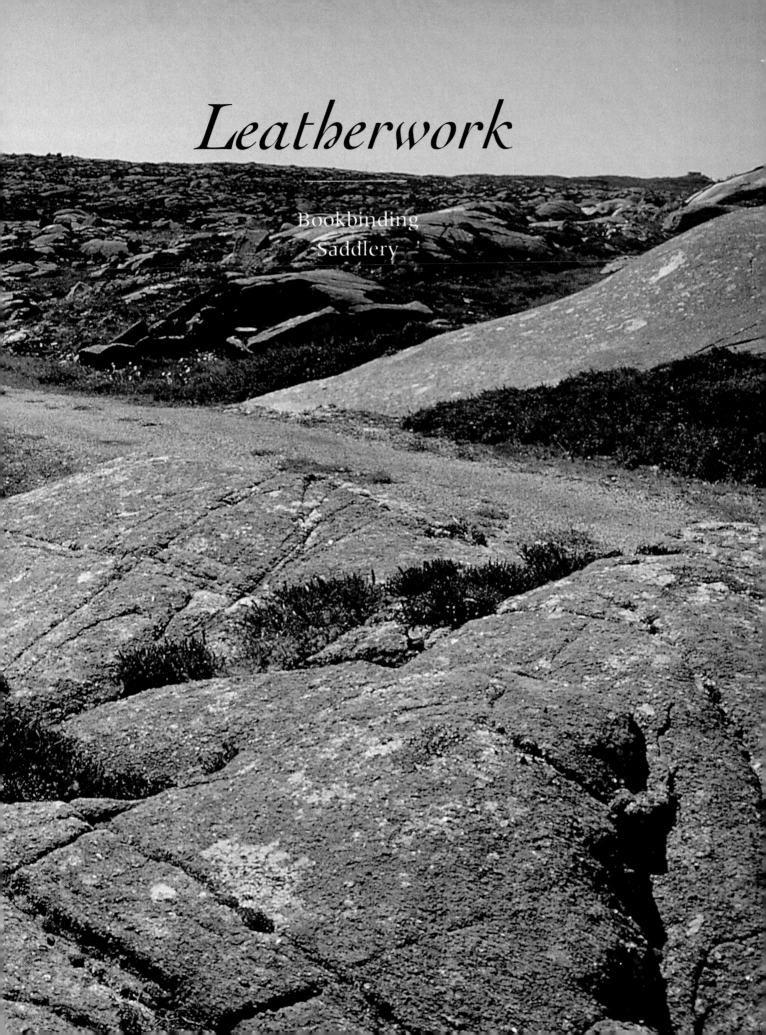

Leatherwork

Bookbinding
Saddlery

Bookbinding

Bindings or covers to protect written or printed matter have always followed the shapes of the material they are protecting. The 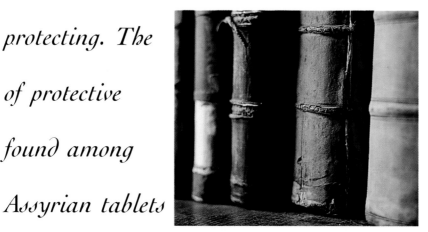 earliest instances of protective covers are to be found among the smaller Assyrian tablets of about the eighth century B.C. These tablets recording sales of slaves, loans of money, and other day-to-day matters, were often enclosed in an outer shell of the same shape and impressed with a short title. Egyptian papyrus rolls were generally kept in roll form bound around with papyrus tape and often sealed with seals of Nile mud; and the rolls, in turn, were sometimes preserved in rectangular hollows cut in wood. The diptychs are the prototypes of the modern book. From about the first to the sixth centuries, ornamental diptychs were made of carved ivory, and presented to important personages by Roman consuls. The method of folding vellum into pages seems to have been first done around the fifth century. The sheets were folded once, and gatherings of four or more folded

erings of four or more folded sheets were made, so that stitches through the fold at the back would hold all the sheets together and each leaf could be conveniently turned over. Very soon man, ever ingenious, thought of an obvious plan of fixing several of these fastenings or quires together; this was followed

*Books ready for rebinding with some of the tools
required for the process.*

by the simple expedient of fastening the threads at the back around a strong strip of leather or vellum held at right angles to the line of the backs. This early method of sewing books is used today in the case of valuable books; it is known as flexible work and has never been improved upon.

As soon as the method of sewing quires together in this way became accepted it was found that the projecting boards at the back needed protection, so that when all the quires were joined together and so far finished, strips of leather were fastened all over the back.

The leather strip soon evolved and covered the whole of the boards (it was called "whole" binding) and it was quickly found that these fine flat pieces of leather offered a splendid field for artistic decoration.

The first ornamentation of leather bindings was probably made by means of impressions from small metal points or lines pressed upon the leather.

English binders excelled in the art of blind stamping, that is, stamping without the use of gold leaf. Such bindings reached perfection during the twelfth and thirteenth centuries at Durham, Oxford, and Cambridge. The Winchester Domesday Book of the twelfth century is one of the best examples remaining today.

From about the seventh to the sixteenth

century illuminated manuscripts were held in high esteem. The exquisite calligraphy and miniature paintings inside were echoed in the outside coverings—beautiful work in metals with jewels, enamels, and carved ivory, dating from the seventh century. The Gospels of Charlemagne, the Stowe Missal, the Book of Kells at Trinity College, Dublin, are just some of the examples of the work of the craftsmen of that period.

In about the middle of the fifteenth century, printing was introduced into Europe, and this brought a reaction against the large, beautiful, and valuable illuminated manuscripts and their equally precious covers. Printing brought small books, cheap books, and ugly books, usually bound in calf, goatskin, or sheepskin. Also in the fifteenth century a new art came into being, the art of gold-tooling on leather, which in the hands of some craftsmen became a great art. Specimens of the work of a few great masters are now highly prized by collectors.

The art of gold-tooling on leather was probably brought to Venice from the East— the finest examples are to be found in late fifteenth-century work. Thomas Berthelet, a Royal Binder to Henry VIII, would appear to be the first binder to practice it in England. The practice of ornamenting English royal books with heraldic designs, which is thought to have begun in the reign of Edward IV, has continued to this day.

For Henry II of France much highly decorated work in binding was done. Richly gilded and colored, these bindings bore the King's initials and the initials of the Queen, Catherine de Médicis, and the emblems of crescents and bows.

Italian bindings, which were made for popes and cardinals, are of high standard, although later Italian bindings were disappointing.

In the reign of Charles I, the niece of a binder Nicholas Ferrer, Mary Collect and her sister, set up what is possibly the earliest commercial bindery in a village in England. They made large scrapbooks, harmonies of the Gospels with illustrations

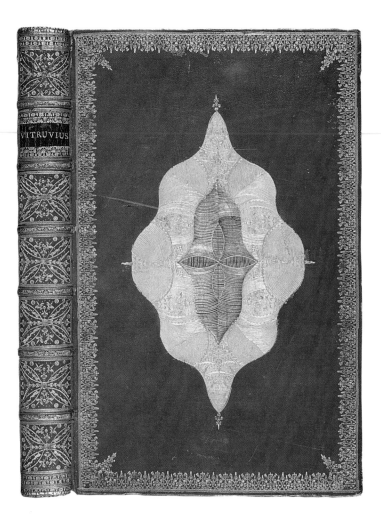

Irish binding, c. 1750, by an unknown craftsman. This is a good example of the high standard of craftsmanship produced in Ireland in the eighteenth century.

and bound them in velvet stamped in gold and silver.

No history of bookbinding is complete without acknowledging the exquisite bindings produced in Ireland during the eighteenth century.

There is no real knowledge of what early bookbinding in Ireland was like. It is on record that elaborately carved service books adorned the altars in early Christian times, and individuals are named as being skilled in the craft, but there is very little material by which to establish a link between the leatherwork of early Christian Ireland and the Irish bookbindings of the eighteenth century. As far as is known no medieval Irish bookbinding has survived.

It was in the late seventeenth century that bookbinding in Ireland emerged as a fully developed craft. The most magnificent bindings produced in Ireland during the eighteenth century were undoubtedly the Parliamentary Bindings. To quote C. D. Hobson, an authority of international eminence, they were "probably the most majestic series of bound volumes in the world."

It is nothing short of tragic that this incomparable series of books which were held in the Record Office of the Four Courts, the seat of Irish law, should have perished as a result of fire in the Civil War of 1922. It was a stroke of fortune that Sir Edward Sullivan, scholar and amateur bookbinder, had twenty-six of them photographed and took rubbings of many more. These are now in the National Library.

In this age of paperbacks and machine-binding the art of the bookbinder still has a role. The demand arises from, among other things, student theses, papers for law libraries, company reports, etc., but also from a public which, generally speaking, has been brought up to believe that the contents of a book are more important than its cover, but now are beginning to appreciate that bookbinders are a rare breed who, from the exercise of their craft, can, among other things, repair a favorite tome or transform a much-loved first edition, which from constant use has become tattered and torn, into a book to be treasured for life.

Statistics show that there has been an increase in the number of people in Ireland and Britain who have given up a variety of other careers in order to learn the ancient craft of bookbinding.

Marsh's Library

Marsh's Library in Saint Patrick's Close, Dublin, is one of Ireland's treasures. It was built in 1701 by Archbishop Narcissus Marsh to a design by Sir William Robinson, and is a magnificent example of a seventeenth-century scholars' library.

The library houses four main collections, consisting of 25,000 books relating to the sixteenth, seventeenth, and early eighteenth centuries. There are books on law, medicine, science, travel, mathematics, music, and classical literature, as well as Bibles in almost every known language in all the collections. Such collectors were true Renaissance men, and their knowledge was wide and varied.

Dr. Muriel McCarthy has been working at Marsh's Library for more than twenty-five years. She is the first woman to be appointed Keeper of the Library since its foundation in 1701. In 1980 she had an honorary degree conferred on her by Trinity College, Dublin, and was

made an honorary life member of the Royal Dublin Society in 1990. The Lord Mayor of Dublin gave her the Millennium Award in 1988 for outstanding achievement. Such a pedigree suggests a rather formidable image; in reality, Muriel McCarthy is a woman of exceptional charm and generosity of spirit, as instanced by her readiness, at short notice, to meet me in the library to talk about conservation and bookbinding.

With admirable foresight Archbishop Marsh placed the library on the top floor of the building, thus ensuring that the books would be safe from damp and mildew. The main entrance to the library is on this floor, and to reach it one walks up granite steps which are part of a thoughtfully planned, lovingly tended garden of mainly seventeenth-century plants—lilies, lavender, rosemary, and several varieties of old roses to name just a few. The seventy-five-foot-long first gallery is entered through an oak door. Carved lettered

Carved letter curtains at the end of the oak shelves in the library are an ornate substitute for the usual labeling system. Cages are topped by a bishop's miter at the L-shaped end of the second gallery. Readers were locked in here when looking at rare volumes.

pelmets, or valances, at the ends of the bookshelves are an ornate substitute for a labeling system.

At the end of the second gallery are three wired alcoves, or cages, where in earlier times readers of precious books were locked to prevent them from stealing the volumes. Its most impressive features are the beautiful oak bookcases and their elaborate pierced pediments which almost reach the ceiling. At the top of each is a bishop's miter.

In 1988 the Delmas Conservation Bindery was opened as an important appendage to Marsh's Library. It is a specially designed building in the garden of the library. Together with its equipment and furniture, it

Sarah McCartan, conservator and bookbinder, sewing the gatherings of a book together on a sewing machine, similar to one used by a twelfth-century monk.

was donated by the late Jean-Paul and Gladys Delmas of New York.

There is a quiet, unhurried atmosphere in the rooms where the binders work, and the sweet smell of glue drifts in the air. Sarah McCartan is sitting on a bench sewing the gatherings of a book together on a sewing frame. The traditional design of the sewing frame is the same as that used by twelfth-century monks.

Olive Murphy, her co-worker, shows me how, as the first stage of the restoration program, the condition of each book is cataloged on a detailed specification sheet.

They are then divided into four types according to their bindings: leather, vellum, cloth, paper.

There was a time when the apprenticeship to bookbinding took seven years, but now it has been reduced to three and a half years. In keeping with a craft that evolved with carefully guarded trade secrets and a long apprenticeship, division of labor was strict. Sewing the pages and the headbands was women's work and required skill, making the case of leather or cloth, trimming and finishing was for men; now two thirds of bookbinding students are female.

Muriel explains the process.

Whenever rare books are being repaired and rebound there are serious bibliographical problems to confront. These include the preservation of annotations, signatures, and other characteristics. For these reasons the preservation of rare books may have to be limited to dry cleaning the marginal areas and stabilizing the text and binding. A book can be placed in a specially designed box which helps to protect its unique features. These conservation boxes are not simply boxes, but are specially made to fit the book. If the book moves around inside the box, or if it is too light, the book will be damaged. Restoration must always conserve and not harm the book's history.

Most of the books in Marsh's Library were printed and bound before 1700. Books which were produced at this early stage were usually printed on superb handmade paper and bound in natural tanned leathers. Because leather consists of bundles of fibers, its suppleness is due to the fact that fiber bundles slide over one another. In the original manufacturing process oils and fats were added in order to preserve the suppleness of the leather. After four hundred years the oils and fats have hardened and lost

their lubricating characteristics and the leather on the books has turned powdery and begun to disintegrate.

When books chosen for rebinding have originally been bound in the sixteenth and seventeenth centuries the binding techniques used at that period are used again. Although in most cases the original leather on the books was smooth calf, it was decided to rebind the books with tested Oasis Nigerian Goat, as it is now impossible to purchase calf of the same quality as that produced in the sixteenth and seventeenth centuries.

Muriel pays tribute to John Gillis of Trinity College Library, her conservation consultant and also to the American Ireland Fund (now the Ireland Fund) which, in 1981, undertook major restoration of the building. The bookcases were cleaned and waxed, and the gold lettering and ornamentation restored. The library was re-wired and many new facilities were added.

The Delmas Bindery, which has carried out such significant conservation on the seventeenth- and eighteenth-century collections in Marsh's Library, also accepts orders from other libraries, institutions, and individuals who are seeking to preserve this unique part of Ireland's great cultural heritage.

Saddlery

How and when horses first came to Ireland is lost in the mists of time. Bones of small ponies have been unearthed at Newgrange, the Neolithic burial chamber in County Meath, dating from around 2500 B.C. The mild climate and the quality of the soil, together with the natural affinity of the Irish people with the horse, have produced an animal of exceptional caliber. The first indication of horses being domesticated came from the epic cycles. The Gaelic heroes used to sortie in chariots drawn by two horses; no mention of riding was made. It is known that horse racing was a popular sport in Ireland from pre-Christian times; the first steeplechase race took place in Buttevant, County Cork, in 1752.

Races were also run at the Curragh in County Kildare; in fact, cuirreach *is the word for racecourse in old Irish.* The earliest illustration of a man on horseback is in the Book of Kells, written in the eighth century

A.D.; *he is depicted with a bridle but no saddle. Although the Celts had taken up riding at an earlier date, the saddle came into its own with the arrival of the Normans in 1171. They came at the behest of Diarmaid MacMurrough, king of Leinster, to teach the art of*

warfare to the people. Up to this period the horses used for warfare and hunting were small, light, and fast. These small horses came to be called hobbies, perhaps the origin of the term "hobbyhorse."

Norman horses were large and powerful—they had to be as they carried soldiers clad in armor who used both saddles and stirrups.

The Norman knight in armor was to the twelfth century what the modern day battle tank is to the present era. These Norman horses changed the face of Irish agriculture, for from the Middle Ages onward they gradually replaced oxen in the field. Around this time also communities began to settle in one place, thus enabling many craftsmen, including harness makers and saddle makers, to make a niche for themselves in a well-organized community, pastoral to a remarkable degree. Throughout the development of both the harness and saddle, two traditions of manufacture were apparent: the landed gentry could afford to pay craftsmen to make saddles, bridles, and

sets of harness; the man with the small holding made his own with wooden bits and súgan (straw) ropes.

The next notable change came with the arrival of the Tudor plantations. A form of organized hunting was introduced, and as by now the wolf was almost extinct in Ireland, the fox was prey for the first time.

Ladies took part in the hunt, riding sidesaddle, and quality harnesses in doeskin were much in demand. Some illustrations from that time show that the Irish still used no stirrups, and the Irish bits and saddles differed a great deal from the English variety.

During the eighteenth and nineteenth centuries road networks improved considerably throughout most of the country; this heightened the demand for coach builders, wheelwrights, and harness makers. From illustrations of that period it can be seen that horses wore full-collar harnesses of the finest quality. With the advent of the motor car, the demand for driving harness declined.

Berney Brothers

The firm of Berney Brothers of Kilcullen, County Kildare, founded in 1850 (their letterhead at that time read: "Racing, Hunting and Military Saddlers and Harness-makers to the Carriage trade") continues to provide specialized saddlery for racing, hunting, dressage, and show jumping. New designs are promoted by riders taking part in international show jumping and dressage. They have a thriving export business to the United States, almost every country in Europe, and Japan; the latter, after centuries of using only samurai saddles, now seems to be inclining toward the European variety.

The techniques of harness and saddle making have changed little throughout the last century. Berneys uses only the best quality leather, which in its turn demands the highest qualified craftsmanship. Their shop at Kilcullen is an Aladdin's cave where if one is interested in horses, one can browse for hours. If you are in a hurry or want something in particular it is best to ask for help, as only the staff (almost, if not entirely made up of members of the Berney family) can, from the apparent chaos, instantly find what you are looking for.

The workshops at the back of the shop contain Berneys of various generations—fathers, sons, uncles, cousins, they are all here, and as far as one can see, all dedicated to their work. In conversation with them it is obvious that they are aware of the responsibility involved in following a long tradition of excellence. The smell of leather and saddle oil pervades the workshop. To one side beneath the window several substantial sewing machines are in use. Jim Berney tells us that they have been in use for seventy years,

Marking out saddle flaps prior to cutting them (below and right).

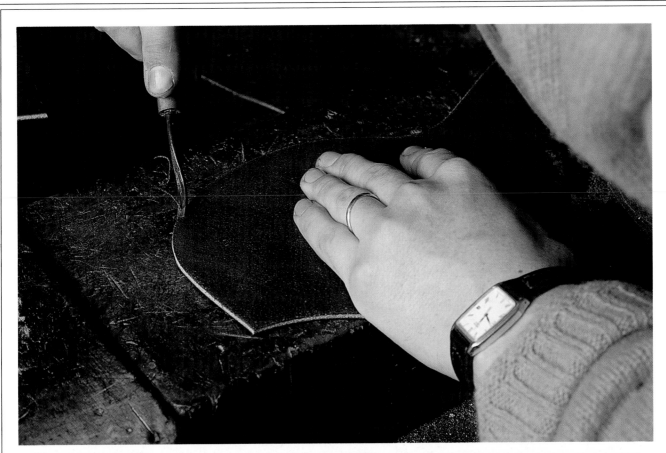

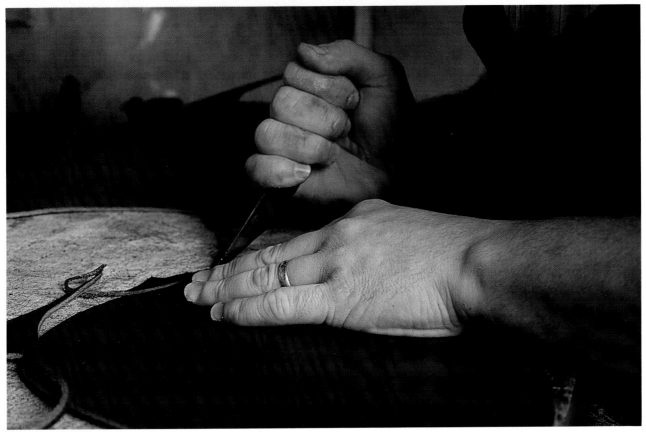

Saddle making: Stuffing a panel.

Using a tack hammer.

Using a pricking wheel.

Stitching on a 1920s sewing machine.

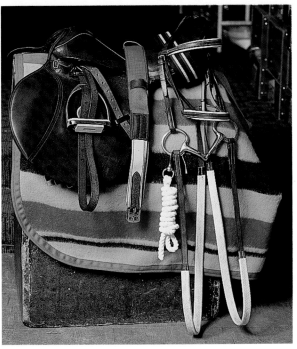

Almost complete, saddles hanging in the workshop.
Show-jumping saddle with bridle and fittings.

and indeed, on their black cast-iron flanks, 1920 is clearly marked, but better machinery for the job has yet to be invented.

Competing with the whirr of the machines is the sound of sharp knives slicing leather. There are no women involved in any of the processes, just men cutting templates, sewing, handstitching, putting to use the various tools of their craft as their fathers and grandfathers did before them.

Acknowledgments

I wish to thank the following people:

Harriet Bell, my editor, for her unfailing encouragement and patience.

Mairead DunLevy of the National Museum, Dublin, for compiling a list of books on Irish crafts.

John Teahan, Keeper of the Art and Industrial Division of the National Museum of Ireland, for his unfailing assistance to me in all matters pertaining to crafts, silver in particular.

The Irish Folk Life Division of the National Museum, Anne O'Dowd in particular.

Wesley Grahame of the National Museum, who helped choose the early Bronze Age gold photographs.

Howard Temple, Chairman of Magee & Co., Donegal, who put at my disposal the thesis on Irish handwoven tweed written by his late niece, Rosemary Harris, which was of incalculable assistance to me.

Muriel McCarthy, Keeper of Marsh's Library, for her generosity.

Cyril McDonnell of the National Dairy Council, for his kind assistance in all matters pertaining to Irish Farmhouse cheeses.

Mary Dowling, for sharing with me her vast knowledge of Irish crafts.

Cyril Cullen, for sharing his knowledge about the history of knitting.

Professor Peter Harbinson, for giving me a copy of *Bechbretha*, an old Irish law tract on beekeeping.

The Ulster Folk and Transport Museum for their information on Irish linen.

Richard Dormer for the photographs on pages 82, 87, 128, 140, and 144.

My deep gratitude to John Connolly for his endless patience.

And finally David Davison, whose enthusiasm is matched only by his talent, is responsible for the photographs that illustrate the crafts, and to the craftsmen and women whose beautiful work made this book possible.

The following are the books and resources which have provided me with most information and inspiration:

Ida Grehan, for her book on Waterford Glass.

David Shaw-Smith, for having written *Irish Traditional Crafts,* which surely must be the encyclopedia of Irish crafts.

Department of Irish Folklore, References: MS 1139, 270; MS 947, 100; MS 283, 9; MS 302, 92; MS 1137, 226. MS 970 and MS 1639, 329.

Cheese: History and the Development of the Irish Cheese Industry by John McCarthy.

Land of Milk and Honey by Brid Mahon.

Osier Culture and Basket Making, by Patrick Smith.

The Irish Heritage Series 27—Irish Pottery and Porcelain.

The Irish Heritage Series 6—Irish Book-binding.

The Irish Heritage Series 21—History of Lace.

Patrick V. O'Sullivan, Article on Kenmare Lace, Irish Arts Review.

The National Museum of Ireland, Dublin, for the pottery photograph (page 6) and the gold and silver photographs (pages 152, 153, 154).

Craftspeople

1. **Tipperary Crystal**
   Ballynoran, Carrick-on-Suir
   Co. Tipperary
   Tel. (051) 41188
   Mouth-blown handout lead crystal

2. **Joe Shanahan**
   Chapel Street, Carrick-on-
      Suir
   Co. Tipperary
   Tel. (051) 40307
   Willow baskets

3. **Hugh O'Neill**
   Tiernee
   Lettermore, Co. Galway
   Tel. (091) 81239
   Master thatcher

4. **Juliet and Paddy Berridge**
   Adamstown, Co. Wexford
   Tel. (054) 40560
   Cheesemakers

5. **Paddy Murphy**
   Hillview Potteries
   Carly's Bridge
   Enniscorthy, Co. Wexford
   Tel. (054) 35443
   Terra-cotta garden pottery

6. **Nicholas Mosse**
   Nicholas Mosse Pottery
   Bennetsbridge,
      Co. Kilkenny
   Tel. (056) 27105
   Pottery

7. **Mary Landy**
   Ballinabranna
   Milford, Co. Carlow
   (0503) 46285
   Rush baskets

8. **Helena Ruuth**
   Lansdown, Church Rd.
   Bray, Co. Wicklow
   Tel. 286 1725
   Handwoven throws and stoles

9. **Berney Brothers**
   Kilcullen, Co. Kildare
   Tel. (045) 81225
   Saddlery

10. **Donald MacPherson**
    26 St. Aidan's Park Ave.
    Fairview, Dublin 3
    Handbeaten gold and silver

11. **Una de Blacam**
    29 Raglan Road
    Dublin 4
    Tel. 688 9196
    Gold jewelry

12. **Marsh's Library**
    Dr. Muriel McCarthy
    St. Patrick's Close
    Dublin 8
    Tel. 543511
    Bookbinding

13. **Irish National Museum**
    Textile Department
    Kildare St.
    Dublin 2
    Tel. 661 8811
    Printed fabrics

14. **Bridget Byrne**
    Ardcalf
    Slane, Co. Meath
    Tel. (041) 24354
    Rush baskets

15. **Carrickmacross Lace**
    Sister Enda McMullen
    St. Louis Convent
    Carrickmacross,
       Co. Monaghan
    Tel. (042) 27105

    Martha Hughes
    Creevy Oliver
    Carrickmacross,
       Co. Monaghan
    Tel. (042) 62506
    Handmade lace

16. **Clones Lace**
    Mamo McDonald
    The Diamond
    Clones, Co. Monaghan
    Tel. (047) 751051
    Handmade crocheted lace

17. **Irish Linen Guild**
    Belfast, Northern Ireland
    Irish linen

18. **Magee and Co.**
    Donegal, Co. Donegal
    Tel. (073) 21100
    Handwoven tweeds

19. **Tommy Daly**
    Celtic Weave China
    Cloghore
    Ballyshannon, Co. Donegal
    Tel. (072) 51844
    Fine bone china

20. **Cyril Cullen**
    Carrick-on-Shannon,
       Co. Leitrim
    Tel. (078) 20100
    Knitwear

21. **Tarlach and Aine de
       Blacam**
    Inis Meáin, Aran Islands
    Tel. (099) 73009
    Knitwear

22. **Kenmare Lace**
    St. Clare's Convent
    Kenmare, Co. Kerry
    Tel. (064) 41385
    Appliqué lace

23. **Veronica Steele**
    Milleens
    Eyeries
    The Beara Peninsula,
       Co. Cork
    Tel. (027) 74079
    Cheesemaker

Index